MAKE *the* Vow, KEEP *the* Vow

Commitment Required

M.L. & ARIAN MOORE

A Prayer for Marriages

Dear God,

We thank you for being the God of Abraham, Isaac and Jacob. We also thank you for being the God of every couple that believes in your Son, Jesus the Christ! We thank you Father that you hear us when we pray. We come to you on behalf of every couple that reads this prayer. We adore you and magnify your name! Thank you for grace and mercy by which we are saved and kept!

First, God, we repent of our sins for we all have fallen short of your glory. May every married couple come to you with a heart of humility and repentance. We all have made mistakes, but thank you Lord God that we are forgiven. We pray now, shepherds leading your sheep, that you would not only have mercy on every couple, but that, Father, you would unify them as one.

May they understand the mystery of being one and that this is the result of your miraculous work – the two becoming one. May they understand that this is the work of the Holy Spirit and it is a work in progress. May every couple seek to be made whole individually as they become one in you. May they lift up one another and help one another where each is weak, that together, they may be whole.

May the love, romance and passion continue in their marriage as it were in the beginning. May they look to you, Lord Almighty, to discover what real love is all about. May they be attentive to one another's needs. May they pray in the Spirit daily, that they are filled with your wisdom to endure and discern what it takes to make their marriage successful.

Now, Father God, we call divine purpose forth in their life together! May they experience Joy unspeakable! Lord, let the success of their union, whether it be offspring, businesses, ministry, etc. bring you much Glory! May it cause other couples to pattern after them and seek your will and your way, in their marriage. Ultimately, may it get the attention of lost souls, whereas, they inquire of the Lord's salvation and His prosperity!

Now unto Him who is able to keep us from falling and present us faultless before His Majesty, Our God, hear our prayer. Oh God, in Jesus' name, Amen!

Prayer by Bishop Paul S. Morton and Dr. Debra B. Morton
Married December 18, 1976

Dedication

This book is dedicated to every married couple out there trying to make it work. We also dedicate this book to each and every person that contributed to the book in any way. We are so grateful for your testimonies and the inspiring advice you had for other couples. This is your book.

Lastly, we dedicate this book to our children. It is our hope that our dedication to one another would set an example for you of true love and commitment founded on the love of Christ.

Introduction

OUR STORY

Our story began on a brisk, morning in March. Arian was home from spring break, a senior at Howard University and M.L., was then stationed at Naval Station Atlanta. Car troubles led them both to a car dealership where they met on Friday March 11, 2005. Their eyes met and eventually they ended up sitting next to one another. "What connected us?" Arian asks. "The word of God. No really." M.L. had his Bible with him and after noticing it, Arian asked the mechanic to please bring her the Bible she left in the car. "I knew he was my husband the moment I saw him and it was God that told me to get my Bible," Arian explains. M.L. details how he first noticed Arian saying, "I noticed her when she first came in the door and had to say, "Guide thine eyes Lord, guide thine eyes."

While reading the story of Ruth, Arian called her then youth Pastor, Reverend Tejado Hanchell to ask him about a part of the story she did not understand. Once the phone call had ended, M.L. was seated next to Arian and they began to talk about everything from church to current events. M.L.'s car was finished first and as he left he says something told him, "You'll regret it if you don't give that lady your number." He gave her his number and literally sped out of the door. She called, praying that he didn't answer and he didn't so she left a message with her number.

From then on they spoke to each other every day, for hours at a time. A friendship was planted and later love blossomed. They were married on March 11, 2006. Has it been happily ever after? No. There's no such thing. But there has been faith, unconditional love and daily sacrifice and those are the ingredients for lasting marriage. Despite being in their thirties, M.L. and Arian began to notice that so many of their friends were choosing divorce over sticking it out. Thus, this book was written in celebration of their ten year anniversary to demonstrate that marriage can work. It was also written to prepare singles for marriage, offer marriage couples hope and help them keep their vows.

THE BOOK

Marriage is no easy task and in a world that esteems self, it's becoming harder and harder for couples to stay married. We don't have a perfect marriage because we aren't perfect people, but we serve a perfect God and by keeping Him first we can perfectly carry out our vows. The goal in us writing this book is not to say that we are experts or that we have the perfect marriage or even that we have it all figured out, rather our goal is to share our experiences and how we make it a daily habit to choose one another.

In each chapter you will find a 'hers' section and a 'his' section where we both share our experiences from our perspectives on specific topics. You will also find a vow for you and your spouse to make as well as a poem. One of the most unique aspects of this book is that we called on a number of couples to also share their experiences and advice. Some are people that we know and some are people that we don't know but the commonality that we all share is that we have made a commitment to stay married. Some of these couples have been married for a little over a year, while others a lifetime.

At the end of the day, all we really have is a commitment towards each other. Marriage is not about perfection, it's about unconditional love and choosing to show that type of love every day. Every marriage is different but what each marriage should have is two people who love God and are willing to do the work to make the marriage work. There's no secret or no one size fits all approach to marriage. What makes marriages last is an undying commitment and unconditional love fueled by Christ's example.

It is our goal that this book will inspire you to keep the vows that you made. It's easy to get married, but the prize is in staying married. Let's dive in!

Table of Contents

CHAPTER ONE

Groundwork

Hers

There are two components that should be in place before marriage; a dedication to God and friendship. I would say that these two ingredients have made our recipe for marriage last. We started out as friends first and that foundation is the basis for our relationship. Being a friend means that we developed trust for each other and developed a true 'like' for one another long before we became intimate or dove into a relationship.

When we met I was a senior at Howard University and I was home for the Spring break. We met at a car dealership and from that moment we have talked to each other every day since. When I went back to school to end the semester and my college career, we would be on the phone for hours. We'd talk about everything, from our childhoods to having Bible study. At the time it was not necessarily agreed upon that

Marriage is sustained through God, friendship, communication, laughter, forgiveness, and support. In every trial that we have encountered, I have learned that it brought us closer to God and helped us learn more about ourselves. To further develop our friendship, we make time for each other and we allow the other person to talk without judgment.

DERRICK & LEKEISHA JACKSON, MARRIED JUNE 24, 2006

2

we would move forward in a relationship (though I knew he was the one). We were content being friends and spending three and four hours on the phone each day. I learned a lot about him and I liked what I saw and heard.

Because we had the opportunity to be friends first, that friendship is often what I defer to when things are rocky in our relationship. I genuinely want what's best for him because he's my friend first. I enjoy being around him. He's more than my husband and my lover, he's my friend. You don't just turn your back on your friend. When your friend is hurting, your goal is to help them. There have been times where I was hurt and wanted more than anything to just leave but my love for him and our friendship keeps me grounded. Being each other's friend means that we respect one another, we dream together, we explore together, we open up to each other and share our innermost feelings regardless of how uncomfortable it may be.

Now that may not be the testimony for everyone—that you started out as friends. Maybe you hooked up on social media and started dating right away. You can still develop a friendship while in a relationship. Friendship is very much so a part of the glue that holds marriage together. A research study from the Gallup Organization discovered that 70% of overall marital satisfaction came from the couple's friendship. The study goes on to indicate that emotional intimacy in marriage was more important than physical intimacy.[1] It's the idea that someone is concerned with your overall well being that keeps the fire burning in a marriage.

How do you develop and maintain a friendship in marriage? The first thing is taking time out for each other. Friends connect. Time may

---

1   Rath, Tom. Vital Friends: The People You Can't Afford to Live Without (Gallup Press, 2006)

look different for each couple depending on the family size or busyness. Start with a morning connection moment, which could be prayer or a cup of coffee. Ask your spouse how their day was when they get home from work. This is one element we added to our marriage that really helped us connect. It allowed me to see into his day and him to see into mine. The other element that really helped us build and maintain our friendship is laughter and not taking life so seriously. When we lost our laughter, the house seemed cold and dying. *"A cheerful heart is good medicine"* (**Proverbs 17:22**). Watch a funny movie or think about how silly some old arguments were. Tell a joke—do something to lighten the mood and put a smile on each other's face. Have a sense of humor!

Lastly, to develop and maintain a friendship I would say, be loyal and have your spouse's back. This is what real friends do. There's nothing like knowing that you have a safe person to go to with your problems and they will hold tight to those secrets. Not only will they hold your secrets but they will protect you and have your back no matter what! That's what friends are for! Your spouse should not have to worry about you gossiping about him or her to the family or your friends. Your friendship needs to be so solid that no one and nothing but the love of God can pass through.

> After six years of building a friendship, and growing in our individual faith walk, God brought us together. It was natural, not forced. And --- It was real! We both have a unique purpose, but our purpose became stronger as we became one. Friendship laid the foundation for a lasting, purpose driven marriage.
>
> **BRAD & KIMBERLY BLOOM, MARRIED JUNE 1, 1986**

THE FATHER

When I met my husband, or shall I say when I first laid eyes on him, what drew me to him was the fact that he had a Bible at his side. What man brings a Bible to the car dealership? Immediately we connected over the word of God. Now again that may not be your story but no matter how you started, just know that dedicating your marriage to God and keeping Him as the third person in the relationship is so important.

Marriage was created by God and it was created to demonstrate His love (agape) in the Earth therefore, there can be no successful marriage without God. The pot needs the potter to function. It is through God and His word that we are transformed into being more like Him. It's about having a personal relationship with God not just going to church on Sundays. That's the first start to keeping God as the center man in your marriage. How can we love someone else without knowing love? **1 John 4:8** says, "*...for God is love.*"

It is important for couples to know that they need God to be at the center of their marriage. Once that is established, they can make a conscious decision to acknowledge Him in every aspect of their relationship. They do this by having a solid prayer life, being committed to the Word, and seeking guidance from the Holy Spirit, especially during difficult times. When a couple shows grace to each other, makes God the priority, and allow His Word to be the final authority in their lives, He will help them love each other unconditionally. Then they can experience heaven on earth in their marriage.

– DR. CREFLO DOLLAR AND PASTOR TAFFI DOLLAR,
MARRIED DECEMBER 27, 1986

We can keep God as the center of our marriage by seeking Him together, talking about Him, serving Him together and consulting

God and His word on our life and our marriage. One way we honor and commit to God is through our finances. I learned the importance of tithing while attending church in college and have done so ever since. So when we got married, we continued to tithe 10% of our earnings. Not one time have we waivered from that no matter how tight things were, because we truly believe that God honors our giving and that tithing is a demonstration of our dedication to Him as a couple. Other ways that we keep God first in our marriage is by fasting weekly together; it strengthens our spiritual bond but also shows God that we are willing to yield ourselves to Him. And finally, we have a prayer closet allocated in our home. Now as a mom of little ones I rarely get to go in that closet. In fact, I generally pray in the shower or in the bed. Nevertheless, we have a space in our home, dedicated to prayer and seeking the Lord. Moreover, in those times where God felt so far away, those were the times that were rough. Those were the times where there was no peace. He has to be first in our marriage.

FORGIVENESS

Keeping God first helps us to be forgiving which is a requirement in marriage. Why? Because your spouse is going to do things that may hurt your feelings. God's word teaches us that forgiveness is expected and necessary. We are to forgive others because we are forgiven. **Ephesians 4:32** says, "*Be kind and compassionate to one another, forgiving each other, just as in Christ God forgave you.*" Despite our many sins and mistakes God continues to offer us forgiveness and there is no limit on that grace—it does not expire. I remember saying to myself, "I've had about enough of his foolishness." M.L. and I had an argument over something

1. Mastery of the art of forgiveness is imperative in a healthy marriage. We all fall short of the call to be the kind of spouse that honors the covenant of marriage. We all say and do things that we wish we could take back but we can't, so our only solution is to forgive and be forgiven on a daily basis.
2. Forgiveness is a decision; it's an act of the will that is not necessarily natural. We don't have to feel like doing it, we simply have to determine that's the healthiest choice that will ultimately lead to the deepest levels satisfaction and joy. Remember, forgiveness is for YOU, not for the person you're forgiving. If you don't forgive, you are giving tremendous power to the person that has done you harm.
3. The odds of having a successful marriage with a root of bitterness are slim. Unforgiveness creates a wall that keeps love out and creates greater and greater distance between mates. Eventually, the distance grows into a coldness that destroys a relationship.
4. There are two levels of forgiveness, both of which have personally served me well. I have had to forgive my exes so that I could be free of my past. If I weren't able to move on from my past it would limit my ability to love in my present. The other level of forgiveness is my day to day existence with my mate in the present that allows us to continue to give and receive love, like breathing in and out. We have to reconcile our differences constantly. We choose to not be easily offended. This does not mean that we don't feel our feelings, it simply means that when we hurt each other we don't let the hurt go any deeper than the decision to forgive. Some hurts take a little longer than others, but the decision to forgive remains a constant.

ELIZABETH CARROLL (JIM CARROLL), MARRIED JUNE 21, 2009

and he called me "stupid." I felt like I had forgiven him enough and he no longer deserved my grace. But then I was reminded of the fact that God requires more from me. **Colossians 3:13** says, *"Bear with each other and forgive one another if any of you has a grievance against someone. Forgive as the Lord forgave you."* Forgiveness is not an option, it's a requirement and to forgive means that we aren't throwing it back up in our spouse's face. **Proverbs 17:9** (NLT) says, *"Love prospers when a fault is forgiven, but dwelling on it separates close friends."* Don't dwell on the situation, once you and your spouse have discussed it and you both come to a resolve, move on. No one wants to be reminded of their faults over and over again.

One of my biggest struggles in marriage has been extending grace to myself. I set out to be perfect and to do everything right; to keep my husband happy and satisfied. When I would not meet that unrealistic goal, I would be so hard on myself and felt like a failure. As a result, I had a very difficult time apologizing to my husband when I would make a mistake. Somehow I imagined that by not apologizing the issue would magically go away. Finally, I realized that there's no perfection on this side of heaven. I can only commit to waking up every day and giving it my best shot and when I do mess up, I apologize and try to do better the next day.

His

Trust begins at the friendship level and without it there is no friendship at all. Friendship is important for cultivating a trustworthy relationship, because it is at the friendship level that we have the chance to observe whether or not this person will be there through the good and bad life brings our way. That's the markings of a true friend. Friendship for me is knowing that this person has my back, they have my best interest at heart, they support me, they are there for me, they tell me the hard truths, they are willing to love me despite my flaws and they never turn their back on me. These are all qualities that were developed before we moved forward in a relationship.

> Trust is Critical. Before we got married, while we were engaged, we hit a snag (infidelity issue, but not a physical one). It was very painful for us to go through and we separated for a while. I didn't see how the relationship could ever be repaired (But God is able!!!!). After awhile, and repeated apologies from Adil, I decided that I loved him like I've never loved anyone else; that he was special. We were going to work it out. We went to counseling and he helped me slowly rebuild my trust in him.
>
> **ADIL & KIRSTEN AZIZ,**
> **MARRIED JULY 25, 2012**

Our friendship was built first because we had boundaries established long before our relationship. If there are any single (unmarried) people reading this, please note this point. Not being involved sexually helped us tremendously in getting to know one another without having our judgment clouded by sex. Neither one of us were virgins when we met so I'm not trying to make anyone feel like we're the picture perfect couple with halos over our heads—both of us had backgrounds. My wife being in another state played a major role in our ability to become intimate from an emotional and mental stand point first. As a result, I literally fell in love with her over the phone.

☘ ☘ ☘

Friendship is so important in a marriage relationship because that foundation of friendship only intensifies in a marriage. That trust that you develop in the friendship phase is pivotal to the marriage. A man has to trust a woman with his heart. I trust my wife and I believe that she has my best interest at heart so whenever she gives me tough love in the form of advice, I know it's coming from a good place. I know she's not plotting to harm me or that her feedback isn't coming from a place of envy. I know it's well intended. If my wife wasn't my friend first I might have a harder time trusting her with my vulnerabilities and my innermost thoughts. Not everyone is privy to those things but close friends are. Honesty becomes second nature in a friendship and there are no secrets.

FINANCES

Yes that's right, no secrets. I hear so many married guys with the thought that "what she don't know won't hurt her." My question is, how do you know? Spouses have secret accounts, secret credit cards and even secret social media accounts. Why all the secrets? Marriage is giving all and sharing all of you and all that you have. As far as money goes, my stance on it is you don't have any money. It's no longer your money. The minute you get married it becomes our money. Everything is ours. From the beginning my wife and I decided that we would have joint accounts. It all goes in and out of one pot. I hear too many wives saying "I didn't make much this week so I have to ask my husband to help me pay my car note?" Huh? It's a lot of "I," "me" and "my" in that phrase. Again it's ours. Your car is his car. His car is your car. His money is your money. Your money is his money. Now, the world may tell you otherwise, but in the eyes of God the husband and wife are one flesh. **Mark 10:8** says, *"and the two will become one flesh.' So they are no longer two, but one flesh."* (also read **Genesis 2:24**). One! Not two but one! So if we are one then everything we had before getting married now also belongs to our spouse. Not having an understanding of this is the very reason people are running to the court house seeking divorces for money problems. Friends don't let money come between them, they lay it all on the table in honesty. There's no hiding purses in the back of the closet hoping your husband will never find them. One way to avoid confusion is to have a budget and a spending allowance each week for each spouse. Where there is understanding and agreement there is peace.

BACK TO FRIENDS....

Maybe you're already married and you realize that you don't have a friendship. I encourage you to invest time in developing one. The intimacy established in a friendship fuels the marriage. Think about how you and your childhood best friend cultivated your friendship. Maybe you hung out every day after school. Maybe you talked on the phone for hours or maybe you spent the night over their house on the weekends. You both liked the same cartoon. You both liked the same video game and played for hours. You told your best friend everything and you guys were inseparable. The constant in these examples is time. You had to invest time in getting to know that person and this is the same in a marriage. Make time for your spouse, learn about the things that they enjoy and do those things together. That's a start. Intimacy starts in the heart not in the bedroom. And the biggest avenue by which we develop intimacy is through communication.

COMMUNICATION

Often times when we think of communication problems we think of arguments and/or disagreements. But a lack of communication in marriage, which results from what's not being said, keeping your feelings to yourself, not being completely honest with your spouse and doing things behind their back, can also cause major issues. Your spouse is not a psychic or a mind reader. Never expect them to be. If there is something you desire or need, you have to let them know. In addition, be honest with your spouse. Be an open book; that's how friendship is cultivated.

Also, it is important to communicate in a way that is respectful and loving. Every marriage will have disagreements; two different people will have two different perspectives. But it's how you move forward from the arguments that matters. In the beginning of our marriage there was yelling, slamming doors and a whole lot of nonsense. Consequently, we had to learn the hard way that in order to communicate better we had to make some changes. You can't just talk to your spouse any old kind of way. Here is the perfect scripture to handle your communication issues: *"My dear brothers and sisters, take note of this: Everyone should be quick to listen, slow to speak and slow to become angry"* (**James 1:19**). If we are busy listening and if we are not angry, we will have time to digest what our spouse's are saying, take our guards down and be receptive to their perspective. I had to learn that my wife's feelings are valid and that she has a right to feel the way she feels.

As the years progress, our arguments are much less frequent than they were before and one thing I have learned is to fight fair, not calling names or throwing cheap blows. This has continued to be something that I have prayed about because

"Our dumbest fight so far was over a brownie."

when I get upset I can really go there. I tend to become sarcastic with my wife and somehow the competitive nature in me just wants to win the battle. Remember this is not a battle. We are a team. If I win, then my spouse loses and because we are one, then in reality we both lose. Keeping God and His word first is the only sure fire way of helping us communicate effectively because it reminds of us His expectations of us.

GOD

God has a way of reminding us that He desires to be priority in our marriage. There is no marriage without God because there is nothing holding you two together. A couple has to constantly focus on the fact that what they have is nothing without God. That may sound cliché but it's the truth. It happens by renewing your mind every day, getting in God's word and allowing His word to change the way you think. By getting in His word you'll understand that God commands a man to respect his wife and a woman to respect her husband and that they equally submit to one another. **Ephesians 5** is a scripture that is often quoted in Christian circles and many only highlight the portion that says that women should submit to their husbands, but that particular section actually begins saying *"Submit to one another out of reverence for Christ"* (verse 21). Submission is something that we both do; husbands and wives. When we study God's word for ourselves instead of depending on what we have learned in the church, we begin to understand that we are equals; we are a team. We are partners in life and this means that we help one another. If your spouse is struggling to do something, step in and help. If your wife is having a hard day, offer to take over with the kids for her. When I was in college my wife would see my frustration when writ-

A person that grows with God knows that God being present is beneficial to the growth process into adulthood. Then, why not also include him in a marriage? He is full of wisdom. He knows what we need and when we need it. He knew how to repair our broken relationship with him and therefore will know how to repair any broken marriage. Not that we should be preparing for a broken marriage but that we should prepare against it and we can do so by including Him.

MICHAEL & ELIA LAWRENCE,
MARRIED OCTOBER 21, 2001

ing papers and because this is her strong suit she would help me. That's what we do as a team. In God's eyes we are one, so if one of us is falling, we are both falling.

GENDER ROLES

In our house, my wife does majority of the cooking and cleaning. This is not because I believe that she is supposed to do that nor is it because I asked her to do it. It's because she enjoys doing it. She's done it from the day we said "I do." There are no gender roles; you do what works in your home and treat your spouse with respect and honor.

I have a female family member (we'll call her Linda) who works full time, comes home to cook dinner, cleans the kitchen, does the laundry and cleans the house. Linda is literally on her feet all day and her husband does absolutely nothing. While she claims that she has no problem doing those things, I am sure she would be so thrilled if her husband offered to help. Share the responsibili-

> The beauty in a marriage relationship is that it can be customized for each couple. It's a tailor made situation with the common principles of God, love and respect. As far as roles, I believe it's more about meeting the needs of your spouse and doing what makes your spouse feel loved and appreciated. Me personally, I like to set the tone for my husband so that when he comes home from work, he enters into a place of peace. I prepare his meals and keep the house in order. But that's my personal choice, not a designated role because of my gender. I do those things because they speak to my husband's heart. My girlfriend's husband is totally different and he prefers that his wife do other things to demonstrate her affection. Really our role in marriage is to give whole heartedly of ourselves to the other person.
> **CHEESETTE COWAN (CAREY COWAN), MARRIED JANUARY 9, 2012**

ties of the house. Since my wife cooks, I do the dishes. If my wife washes clothes, I will fold them. Has it always been this way? Absolutely not! In fact, through counseling, I began to understand that my wife needed my help. What works for me is a honey-do list. She tells me what she needs done and I got it. It's really not about who does what because of the gender, rather it's about who does what because they are efficient at the job.

Being a good teammate means that you allow your spouse to operate in the lane that best suits them. For a while my wife struggled in understanding that I was not effective at giving the kids baths at night. For whatever reason, I turned into the Grinch at bath time. The kids just drove me up the wall. It took years of seeing this for my wife to realize that it just wasn't working. She came to me randomly with a compromise saying, "I will give them baths every night if you read to them." This is what it means to be equals and partners in a marriage.

The instructions given to husbands are much more elaborate than those given to wives. In fact, I feel like we have more of the responsibility because God holds us responsible for the household. It says, "*Husbands, love your wives, just as Christ loved the church and gave himself up for her…In the same way, husbands ought to love their wives as they love their own bodies*" (**Ephesians 5:25, 28**). **1 Peter 3:7** (NLT) says "*you husbands must give honor to your wives. Treat your wife with understanding as you live together. She may be weaker than you are, but she is your equal partner in God's gift of new life. Treat her as you should so your prayers will not be hindered.*" This scripture is saying that though our wives are physically weaker than we are, she is still our equal and that when we mistreat our wives our prayers are hindered. Think about your mom or your daughter and how you would want a man to treat her. That's how you should treat your wife. Your wife is precious and valuable. You treat something of value differently than you would treat trash. You throw trash out, but something of value, you put it in a safe place to admire it or you put it on a shelf so that others can admire it and see how precious it is. That's how you want to treat your wife in both your words and your actions.

In the end, it all goes back to keeping God first. Our relationship with God helps us to be better friends to our spouse's because we see them through the lens of God's love. God's word helps us to transform our minds from a worldly mindset to a more Christ based view of life. His word helps us better understand that marriage is about giving 100% of ourselves 100% of the time. Even as I write that I am convicted to do more. Like life, marriage is a journey and we are constantly evolving to be more and more like Christ. To evolve and grow together we must keep God first and keep our friendship alive.

THE VOW

I vow to establish and maintain a friendship with my spouse. I understand that friendship is the foundation of our marriage and is what keeps it going. I vow to spend time with my spouse and making that time a priority. I also vow to keep God first in our marriage. I will seek Him daily and we will establish His word as the final authority in our household. God's word declares us to be equals so I will treat my spouse as an equal. I will respect and honor my spouse. I will allow the word of God to transform my thinking and my actions to be reflective of His love in my life and in my marriage.

Be My Friend
By Arian T. Moore

He grabbed my hand
Walked me to the bedroom
Sat me on the bed…
Then he asked me about my day.

I smiled
We talked for a while,
He stood me up,
He kneeled me down…
Then we prayed.

CHAPTER TWO

What is the Vow?

Hers

One of the gravest mistakes people make is entering into marriage without having an understanding of what it is. And it's a shame that many of our perceptions come from television because there is such an unbalanced representation of marriage on the tube. It goes from *Four Weddings* and *Say Yes to the Dress* to *Divorce Court*. This is why pre-marital counseling is so important because it is supposed to define marriage and set expectations for what marriage life will be like. Too often we define our marriage perspective based on what we have envisioned it to be. That's what I did. Marriage for me and many women is a fairy tale. It's a scene out of the pages of a romance novel or a Disney movie. It's flowers every day, romantic trips, wining and dining, passionate love making….forever. That's not at all what marriage is. Marriage is a relationship between a husband and wife established by God and for His purposes. Marriage is a covenant; a binding agreement meant to last a lifetime. Simply put, marriage is a commitment. It's really that simple to explain but much more difficult to carry out. Living in a world where we are told to do whatever feels good and do whatever makes us happy, getting and staying married becomes challenging. Why? Because there are times when marriage doesn't make you feel good and there are times when you are not happy within your marriage.

While my husband and I went through pre-marital counseling and discovered some much needed information, nothing really prepared us for marriage. This is primarily because we were still in that googly eyes phase of our relationship and everything sparkled. While the ministers (a married couple) that counseled us were candid about their experiences in marriage, I was of the thought that "Oh that will never happen to us." On the other hand, I don't think I fully grasped the purpose of marriage and the seriousness of the commitment. The other part of that is nothing really prepares you for marriage. Every marriage is unique and what works for one may not work for another. But the basis of any marriage is the commitment and the understanding that it's you and me through every season, every trial, every misfortune and every victory. The problem is we put so much emphasis on the wedding day and not enough on the marriage.

> In reality, marriage is hard work! We have been married for six months and the articles I read, our pre-talks and all these marriage books have failed me, but there is one thing that has proven to be saving and that is the word of God!
>
> *- DEREK AND QUINAE JACKSON,* **MARRIED AUGUST 14, 2014**

The wedding day. What a blur. Not because I didn't have a nice wedding. We had a beautiful wedding on a bright, sunny day in March at a country club overlooking Stone Mountain here in Georgia. My grandma (rest her soul), touted that it was the most beautiful wedding she had ever witnessed. But I remember so little about that day and it's amazing that people spend thousands of dollars on one day and then look back and can barely remember who was even there. The part that we should remember and pay most attention to is the vows that we spoke. What did we say? What did we promise? The most basic wedding vows go something like this:

"I, ___, take thee, ___, to be my wedded husband/wife, to have and to hold, from this day forward, for better, for worse, for richer, for poorer, in sickness and in health, to love and to cherish, till death do us part, according to God's holy ordinance; and thereto I pledge thee my faith [or] pledge myself to you."

I don't remember promising that and for that reason, there were times in my marriage where I never considered the vows that I made. When I'm going through hard times in life, I can defer back to the promises of God. I can look at His word and reflect on what He said. The same is true in marriage. When my husband has tapped danced on every last one of my nerves or when he has hurt my feelings, I should be able to think back on the promises that I made to him and the promises that he made to me. The vows hold the answer to every issue we will ever face in the marriage relationship. He lost his job and we have no money. But you promised for rich or for poorer. She doesn't appreciate me and takes me for granted. But you promised for better or worse. I don't love him they way I used to. But you promised to love him.

Let's stick a pin right there. Marriage is not about being in this hallucinated, high school kind of love for fifty plus years. Love is a decision. God chooses to love us, every second, every day despite our wrongs and our disobedience. This is the same type of love we are to demonstrate in marriage and it is what we promised in our vows; to choose to love no matter what. Love is a choice, it's not a feeling.

Ephesians 5:1-2 *Imitate God, therefore, in everything you do, because you are his dear children. Live a life filled with love, following the example of Christ. He loved us and offered himself as a sacrifice for us, a pleasing aroma to God.*

John 15:12-13 *This is my commandment: Love each other in the same way I have loved you. There is no greater love than to lay down one's life for one's friends.*

Based on the two scriptures above we are to walk in love and love others the same way that God loves us; laying down our lives for them. In our marriages this is the love we are expected to operate in. This understanding of love takes maturity and an acceptance and understanding that we use God as our example in marriage, not friends or society. It took years for me to understand this. I don't love my husband based on what he does for me, I love him because of the promise that I made. Everything comes down to the vows, the promise.

I took a casual poll on one of my social media accounts and asked my friends to define marriage. Here were the responses:

Marriage is…

- 🕊 Awesome - Fred Matthews

- 🕊 A blessing – Morgan Smith

- 🕊 Worth it - Shenina Dudley

- 🕊 Sacrificial – Jaha Howard

- 🕊 What you make it – Tashiya Umoja

- 100/100 not 50/50 – Orlando Washington

- Work – Jessica Jones

- Ministry – Eve Hughes-Coley

- A blessing in disguise – Lee Gaines

- A journey – Samantha Robbins

- Beautiful – Nathalie Hawkins

- A full time job yet a beautiful work of art, that you're proud of and want to display it's beauty every chance you get – Mignon Hilliard

I think these varied responses are a good representation of all that marriage is. Marriage is indeed all of these things; it's a beautiful blessing that requires work. The work in it is to love and to keep the vows that you made.

His

Marriage is two halves coming together and making a whole and working as a unit. Men and women are uniquely different, both having unique, inherent abilities that complement one another. Rather than remaining weak in an area, marriage gives us the opportunity to be strong in our weak areas through our spouse's. For example, money management was never a strong suit of mine. Money came and money flew out of my hands. My wife on the other hand is disciplined in the area of finances. As a result, I am now strong in an area where I was once weak. It reminds me of **Ecclesiastes 4:9** (NLT) which says, *"Two people are better off than one, for they can help each other succeed."*

Marriage allows us to grow as people. We are forced to address issues within ourselves that have gone awry. You never get to really see your flaws until there is someone else there to point them out. My wife thought she was perfect until she got married. See marriage allows you to see it all. You see the grit, the grime and the sticky stuff that no one else gets to see. My wife often says that I became a different person once we got married. Of course that's not true at all. I just stayed suited and booted while we were dating and then let my guard all the way down after marriage. I was who she thought I was, I just had a few more dents that she didn't know about yet.

This does not mean that we are commissioned by God to change our spouse's, quite the opposite actually. We are commissioned to change ourselves. Too often in marriage we want to change our spouse's into replicas of us. We want our spouse's to think like us, act like us and do things the way we do them. So we criticize them for the way they do something not appreciating their uniqueness. I am still learning this lesson myself, but we have to remember that different does not necessarily mean wrong. My wife may cut an onion differently than I do but that does not make her way wrong. It just makes it different. It is our differences that allow us to complement one another. If my wife was just like me I'd still be weak in the areas where I need strength. Think about it, would you really want someone just like you? Not me, not today, not ever, simply because I can be a pill, but more importantly because I would never grow as a person.

> When we were married, the preacher said "Until Death do us part" and we really stood by that. We just never thought about separating or staying mad at each other. We listen to what each other have to say and if we disagree on something we might discuss it for a while, but we would just drop it and respect each others' opinions. We won't always agree on everything. In a marriage, one person can't be right all the time. If we have a disagreement, we don't let it interfere. We never would go to sleep mad at each other and eventually we would know who was right in an argument in the end. Marriage is life-long and we stand by that.
>
> **HAROLD AND EDNA OWINGS,**
> **MARRIED OCTOBER 24, 1931**

Let's be clear, marriage can kick you in the butt and every day you are working to get better at it. That work helps you grow as a person and ultimately as a spouse. Where there are areas for change it is not us trying to force our spouse's into changing. The fact is, you can't make a grown person do anything. But what you can do is love them, express to them the area that needs addressing and then pray and depend on God to water that seed. God is faithful; trust Him with your spouse. But know that beating your spouse over the head will NOT result in change, only resentment and rebellion against the very issue you approached them with.

Side banter: Speaking of people changing after marriage reminds me of our very first major argument. Now this was a big one. So we had just come home from our honeymoon cruise. Life was grand. My first check came in post marriage and this woman decided to pay all the bills. She paid all the bills, allocated the tithe, got groceries and gas and we only had like $30 left over. I thought the woman was crazy. I simply could not understand what would possess her to pay all the bills to the point that we had no wiggle room. That's just not what I was taught. You move some stuff around to make sure that you have some pocket change. It was hard, but we made it to the next pay day. But see here is where I learned about the importance of being a good steward over your finances. Not only did she pay the monthly bills but she also helped me pay off all my debt. She showed me that there was something to having a good credit score and paying bills on time. Again, that's the value in marriage; there is someone strong in

> Our marriage has lasted mainly by trusting each other. Respecting each other and minimizing arguments by what's right instead of who's right. And not the "I told you so" in your face method. We know a lot about each other but have a lot left to learn about each other also. Peaceful evenings at home are important because you might not get it at work or anywhere else.
>
> **RINALDO MCMATH (SHARON MCMATH), MARRIED NOVEMBER 18, 1989**

areas where you may be weak. I also taught her how to maneuver funds when things got tight…"Call em' up and tell em' we'll put something on it." (My Mama taught me that).

$$\mathscr{D} \ \mathscr{D} \ \mathscr{D}$$

One of the misperceptions of marriage is that your partner is going to make you happy all the days of your life. Where in the H-e-double hockey sticks do people get this idea? Marriage is not a lifetime of bliss. There will be blissful moments but there will be trying moments also. I think people fall short because they don't anticipate the trying moments, they only expect the blissful moments. If more people anticipated the trials, they'd be more apt to tough it out rather than hollering out the D-word.

THE VOW

I vow to understand that marriage is a coming together of two different people. I vow to trust God with my spouse knowing that he alone is able to bind us together in unity. I will not judge my spouse or demean him (or her) for doing things differently because I understand that different does not mean wrong. Instead, I will embrace our differences knowing that those differences allow us to complement one another so ultimately we are imitators of Christ.

Get Happy
By Arian T. Moore

Happiness is not only found in the moments of bliss,
It's found in the apologies and the compromise.
Happiness is not the just absence of trials,
It's also in the overcoming of rough times.
Happiness is not simply romantic nights and late mornings
It's also in the late night prayers and morning revelations.
Happiness is perspective.

BIBLE STUDY 1

CONTRACT VS. COVENANT

Marriage is not a contractual agreement. Marriage is a covenant relationship. In the Bible, the word covenant is used to represent a bond; a promise. In its biblical sense the term means that the two parties are bound to one another. It is a vow we make, not just with the party or parties involved, but with God himself. The marriage covenant is a bond that is to last a lifetime; where the husband and wife cleave to one another and become one flesh (**Genesis 2:24**). Thus the act of two people becoming one means that there is no end. They are forever in covenant with one another.

Jesus elaborated on this covenant saying, *"Have you not read, that He who created them from the beginning made them male and female, and said, 'For this cause a man shall leave his father and mother, and shall cleave to his wife; and the two shall become one flesh?'"* Then Jesus added, *"Consequently they are no more two but one flesh. What therefore God has joined together, let no man separate."* (**Matthew 19:4–6**).

The rituals and symbols established during the wedding ceremony demonstrate that the two parties are entering into a covenant, not a contract. There's the exchanging of vows, witnesses, the changing of the wife's last name, among other symbols. When we exchange vows we make a vow, an oath before God to carry out the very words that we say.

SCRIPTURAL REFERENCES:

For what reason? Because the Lord has been witness between you and the wife of your youth, against whom you have dealt treacherously though she is your companion and your wife by covenant. **- Malachi 2:14**

When you make a vow to God do not delay in fulfilling it. He has no pleasure in fools; fulfill your vow. It is better not to make a vow than to make one and not fulfill it. **- Ecclesiastes 5:4-5**

Contracts expire. A contract has no bounds and is conditional. Think about when you purchase a car and sign the contract; the contract is for three to five years and you are obligated to first qualify for the loan and then carry out the requirements described in the loan, in terms of making payments on time. Eventually that contract expires and you're out of it. It's over. You are no longer obligated to that agreement. Whereas in marriage, there is no expiration date; there are no conditions to you fulfilling the vows that you made. More importantly, where a contract is more about, "what can I get," a covenant asks, "what can I give." Where a contract intends to protect its own assets and interests; a convent is more interested in the concerns of the other party. Where a contract says "I'll do it because I have to;" a covenant says "I'll do it because I want to." Where a contract is willing to meet halfway; a covenant is willing to go all the way. Why? Because the covenant of marriage is based solely on the love of God; a love that has no limits; no conditions and no boundaries.

In **Ephesians 5:32**, Jesus compares the husband and wife relationship to His relationship with the Church (his people). Jesus is bound to us; He laid down His life for us and His love has no conditions.

A contract has conditions and if you don't meet those conditions you face penalties. A covenant says my love has no conditions; I'm going to follow through on my vows even if you don't. Because you and your spouse made a vow before God, He's involved in the relationship. Let Him deal with your spouse. You do your part.

> *"Ask not what can my spouse do for me, but what can I do for my spouse."*

DISCUSSION QUESTIONS:

1. (Singles and Married Couples) How does this understanding of marriage as a covenant change your perception of the marriage relationship?
2. (Married Couples) Were you operating as if you were in a covenant or a contract?
3. (Married Couples) What changes can you make in your relationship based on your new understanding?

****If there is infidelity or abuse involved, this changes the circumstances and in these cases we advise that you seek God and counseling in making the best decision for your family.

THE ALBUM:

Couples that Made the Vow and are Keeping It

Billy & Holly Roesing

Married November 3, 1990
Celebrated 25 years of marriage with a vow renewal service.
Photo Credit: Robert Gabriel Photography

Stephen & Sharonne Murphy

Married October 27, 2013

Joe & Kristen Pinto

Married August 26, 2013

Stephan & Wendy Wright

Married July 10, 2014
Photo Credit: Kesune Stephenso

M.L. and Arian Moore

Married March 11, 2006
Celebrated 10th anniversary with a vow renewal
Photo Credit: Vania Hardtle

Brad & Kimberly Bloom

Married June 1, 1986

Glenn & Michelle Riley

Married June 20, 1996

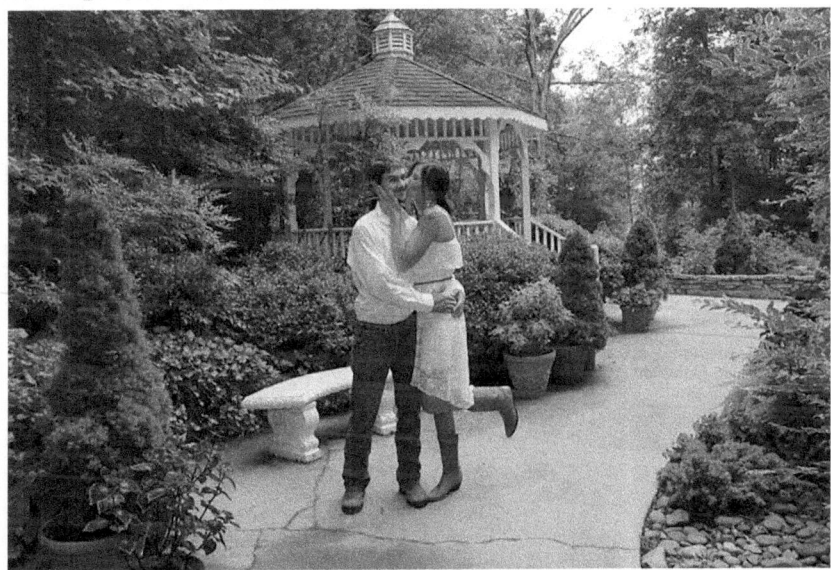

Jason & Wendy Long

Married August 6, 2013

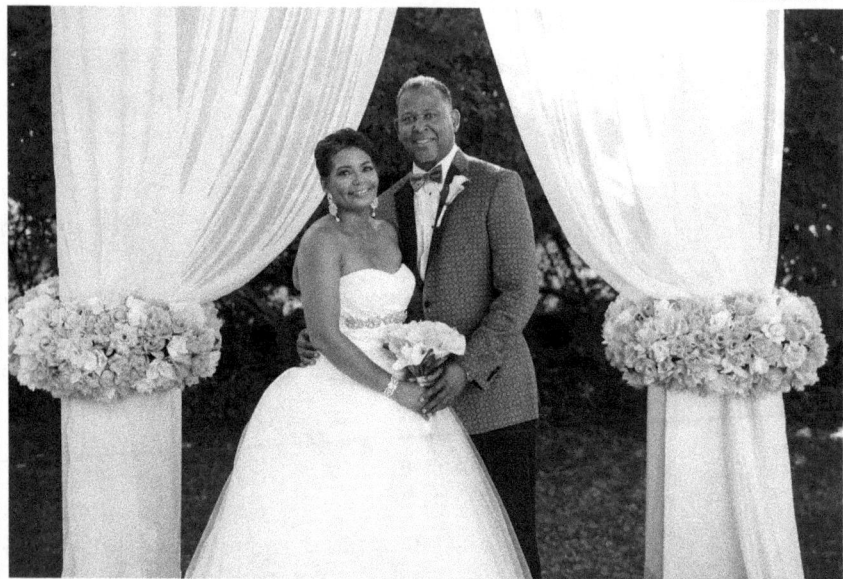

Bernard & Edana Perry

Married July 6, 1985
Celebrated 30 years with a vow renewal wedding ceremony
Photo Credit: The Pros

Travis & Chasity Allcock

Married April 21, 2015

Harold & Pauline Owings

Married October 24, 1931

Quanisha & Michael Williams

Married July 11, 2015
Photo Credit: Mario Nixon

Mark & Charlotte Shue

Married October 24, 1992

Denzyl & Luz Mauras

Married May 10, 1997
Photo Credit: Reynaldo Mauras

Steve & Beverly Williams

Married June 5, 2015

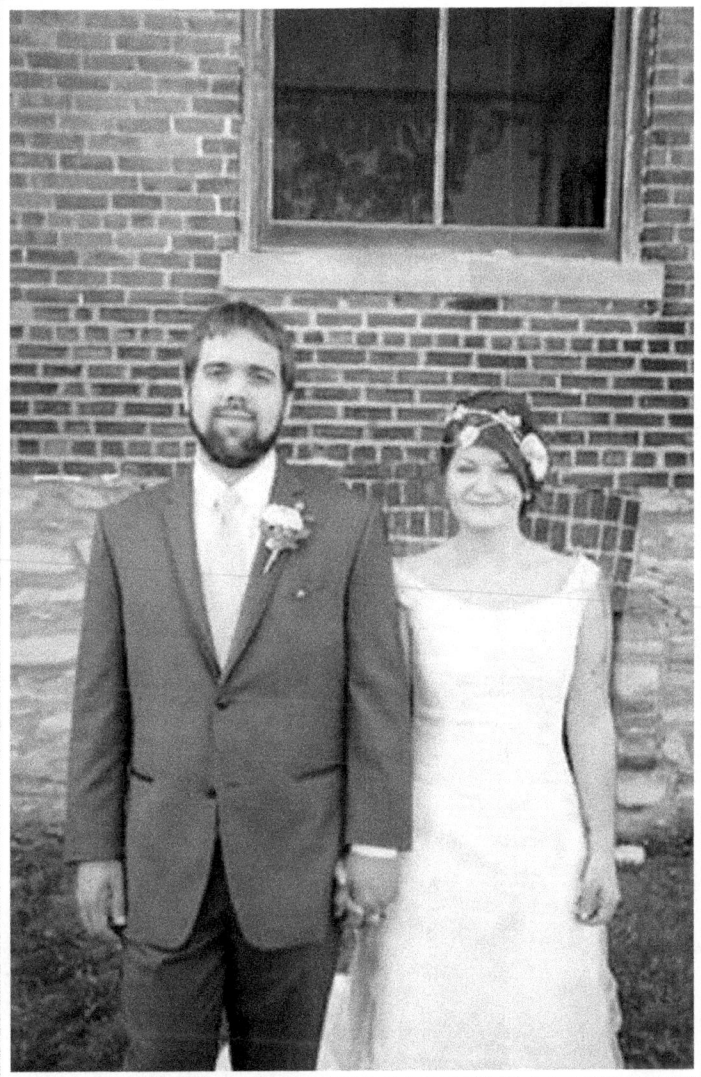

Alex & Brittany Kuhl

Married May 2, 2015
Photo credit: Kate Schwenker

Solomon & Jamila Jefferson

Married June 18, 2011
Photo Credit: Sandra S.

Corey & Channing Bufford

Married September 21, 2014

Danny & Jennifer Pratt

Married March 28th, 2015

Todd & Kimberly Cochran

Married August 27, 1999

Kelvin & Martisha Upson

Married November 16, 2010

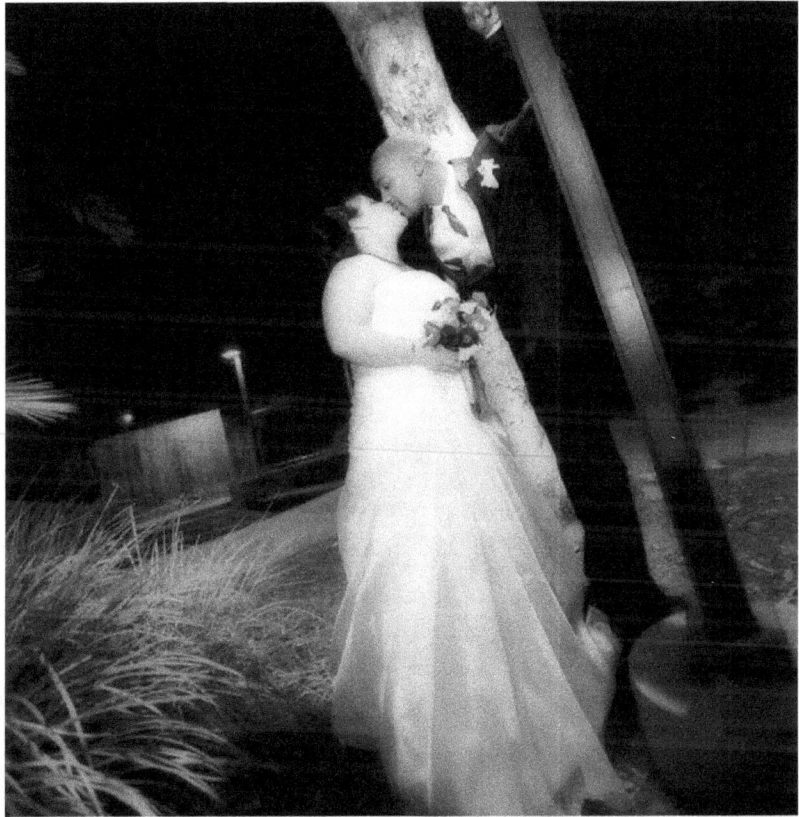

Charlie & Claudia Jackson

Married January 28, 2012

Ricky & Amanda Gonzalez

Married October 24, 2008

Matthew & Vanessa Roark

Married December 6, 2014
Photo Credit: Mallory Ingram

Jarritt & Antonia Sheel

Married April 18, 2009
Photo Credit: Alyssa Aviles Hopkins

Nick & Gina Ferrari

Married October 14, 2015
Photo Credit: Ruth Barral

Clint & Caitlin Smith

Married September 25, 2015
Photo Credit: Victoria Miller

Tamir & Marquietta Reed

Married May 5, 2012

Philip & Susan Camp

Married December 27, 1997
Photo credit: Mixon Photography

David & Cherice Ornelas

Married August 15, 2015

CHAPTER THREE

The D-Word

Hers

There have been a number of times where I felt like throwing in the towel. That's all I knew. My parents separated when I was nine years old and because of that example, it appeared to me that divorce was an option. In addition to my parents, there weren't any solid, consistent examples of marriage around me. I think this made the biggest difference for me and I notice it more now because I see the difference in my husband's perspective on marriage (his parents are still married) and my own. The way we are raised and what we see shapes us and makes us into who we will become. Left unbridled, many of the warped things we were exposed to as children can ultimately ruin our lives and lead to generational occurrences. I believe in my entire family only two people are married and have never divorced. That's out of my parents and a total of 15 Aunts and uncles. Quiet naturally, I went into marriage with a different view. If it doesn't work, I'm out.

Obviously I'm not alone in having those thoughts but there is a difference in having those thoughts and 1) leaving them unchecked and 2) acting out on them. Too many couples are acting out on those thoughts. For years the divorce rate has been 50% meaning that the average marriage has a 50/50 chance of making it. Changing views in society often result in changes in lifestyle. In our society, marriage is no longer deemed as a necessity nor is it considered relevant. Despite that fact, we must keep in mind that we are believers and followers of Christ. With that said, our moral fabric is not determined by the changing waves of a secular world. Rather, our core values are based solely on the word of God and according to His word, marriage was created by Him and no man shall separate what God has joined together (**Mark 10:9**).

Divorce may seem like an easy option but nothing about divorce is easy, not the process and not the ramifications. You don't just go to the court house and fill out paperwork. In fact, it's easier to get married than divorced. It's a long process and if children are involved it can be even longer with custody battles, visitation determinations and the like. There's the petition, notifying the spouse, a temporary hearing, the agreement and then the trial (this may vary by state). Divorce can get ugly and it usually tears families apart. As a child, I will never forget what it was like for me when my parents divorced. I was once close to my dad's side of the family, after the divorce I hardly saw them anymore. My dad was no longer there with me. Don't get me wrong, my dad came around, we spent time together and he paid child support but he was not in the home, he was not present on a daily basis. Most children from broken homes will tell you that the divorce had lasting effects on their lives and the same is true for me.

The other reason for quitting being an option for me after getting married was the fact that we practice it all throughout our dating years; we actually practice divorce. Dating in our society's view has no real purpose—we date just to date. If the end goal in dating is not marriage, what exactly is the point? We get in relationships, most of which we have no business in in the first place, only to break up and then get in a new relationship. By the time we get married we've been in so many relationships that didn't work, and we bring unnecessary baggage into the relationship that otherwise would not have been there. What makes us think that that same mindset won't carry over into marriage? For many, it does because we are so used to having the door as an option. When things go south, instead of sticking it out, our first inclination is to take flight.

The idea of the fairy tale is another thing that led to me wanting to quit. Because I had no examples of marriage I based what I thought marriage was like on what I saw on television and the sweet moments I remembered of my parents while they were married.

> When Susan and Robbie came to see me about a wedding, they said, "Oh, one thing more. We do not want to say, 'Til death do us part.' After all, so many people say that and obviously don't mean it since the divorce rate is so high. We want to be honest." I said, "What do you want to say?" They said, "We want to say 'So long as love shall last.' I said, "That'll be about Tuesday." They said, "What are you saying?" I said, "That there will be plenty of days you despise each other. That doesn't mean you should get a divorce. Your marriage has to be based on something more permanent than how you are feeling at the moment." They said, "So, what do you suggest?" I said, "Til death do us part." Lock yourselves into marriage and throw away the key. If divorce is ever considered an option, your marriage is in trouble.
>
> – *PASTOR JOE MCKEEVER,*
> **MARRIED APRIL 13, 1962**

My parents never argued in front of me so I only have fond memories of them together as a couple. I remember my dad gently washing my mom's hair, massaging the shampoo into her hair. I remember him running her bath water, making the temperature just right and even washing her back. I remember him willingly helping out around the house, cooking home-made meals and cleaning. Oddly enough, it was as if he found honor in doing those things and I wanted a man like that. I wanted a marriage like that. They had a fairytale marriage is what I thought. But I was only privy to the highlight reel of their relationship, you know, like what we see from most marriages on social media. We see the smiles and the family portraits, but we don't see the tears and the disagreements, the slamming doors and the name calling.

My views on marriage were based on the goodness I saw in my parents' relationship and what I read in books and saw on TV. I thought that a happy marriage meant that we were always happy, that we never argued, that we were best friends and laughed and had those long passionate kisses every day and he romanced me every day and we forever lived in bliss. Amen. Well as we all know this is not the reality of marriage. In fact, marriage is absolutely nothing like that. Maybe the first year or so but as we begin to take all of the facades off and show the other person who we really are, the real work begins.

There was a specific season of my marriage where I felt like I had just married the wrong person. It seemed that we had nothing in common and even though they were small things, they seemed like mountains. Every time I turned around we were in disagreement over something. He wanted pizza, I wanted Mexican food. He liked strawberry jelly, I wanted peach preserves. He wanted to spend every Sunday relaxing on the sofa watching the football game; I wanted to spend Sundays together exploring and creating memories. It was like we were off. In my mind nothing was clicking, nothing was perfect. And then it hit me! Nothing about marriage is perfect! Where do we even get this idea that marriage is supposed to be perfect? The people who write those books and produce those movies often times aren't even married. It's a fantasy world! It's not real! What is real about marriage is the commitment to do the work. The Bible says in Genesis, the two shall become one flesh. What does it mean to become? That doesn't happen on the honeymoon night. It's through a constant coming together and working through issues that we become one flesh. We complement each other in such a way that where he is weak, I am strong and vice versa.

That's not to say that I still don't struggle with this. Even as I type this sentence I recall an argument that cut so deep that I felt like we just couldn't go on. I even googled information on separation. I want to be as candid as possible, not because I want to tell all my business, but because I believe that there is healing in transparency. See, even though I took to google, I eventually came out of the flesh and allowed the God in me to have a calm conversation with my husband and we were able to work things out. Ultimately, that's what marriage is about, working it out and sticking it out no matter what you face.

I would like to think also that the devaluing of marriage in our society is another obstacle that makes it hard to maintain a loyal stance on marriage, for both men and women. Women are now taught to be independent, "don't depend on no man for nothing," "you can do bad all by yourself." I guess I had developed an "I can do bad all by myself" mentality. There is no place for this mindset in a marriage relationship. We were created to be helpers to men. So to say that we don't need them is rejecting the very purpose of the male female relationship. **Genesis 2:18** says, *"The Lord God said, "It is not good for the man to be alone. I will make a helper suitable for him." "* We need each other and that's a fact. There is nothing wrong with depending on your spouse, again society and media do not dictate how we conduct our families and our lives. We determine our value system based on the love of God found in His word.

I like to compare marriage to a lifelong car purchase. So you go to the dealership and you buy a car and you make a vow to the car salesman to keep the car until you die and never to part with the car. What are you saying? That even if the car gets dented, even if it's no longer shiny, even if it doesn't perform as it once did, you are keeping that same car. The car is yours until you die no matter what. You can't trade it in. You can't get another one. It's yours because you promised— you made a vow. The same thing applies to marriage and the vows we make on our wedding day. I think even though we recite these words on the wedding day, we are so overjoyed by the occasion that the words just slip out and we don't think and take in what we've said. Those vows were not just a part of the ceremony. We made a vow, a declaration, a promise in front of God and our family and friends. It should not be as easy as it is for us to throw away the promise that we made.

His

M arriage works, divorce hurts. That's simply put, but if I can be real, marriage works if you do the work. Because I grew up in a two parent household, I had the privilege of seeing the good and the bad that happened within my parents' relationship. I saw them working; working on the marriage and working out their differences. Of course there were arguments and some were worse than others, but there was also the unconditional love, the compromise and the forgiveness. I saw that and I wanted that. Through it all they never gave up on one another; they continued to love each other unconditionally in spite of the frustration and pain they might have experienced from life and each other. This example alone is the reason why divorce was never and will never be an option for me, simply because it was never an option for the people that showed me what a marriage is supposed to look like—my Mom and Dad. To this day they remain committed and dedicated to the vows that they made. So I can't speak on why divorce has been an option for me because it's not, but what I can do is talk about some of the reasons people consider divorce and why one should reconsider those reasons.

People get divorces for the most trivial reasons nowadays; sticking it out has become sort of a lost art. If we look at divorce from God's perspective your reason for getting a divorce is trivial, unless of course there is abuse or infidelity. For instance, one of the top reasons people call it quits today is because of financial circumstances. Listen, I understand that when the money is funny it can be an extremely stressful situation because my wife and I have been there and back a few times, but funny money is covered under your wedding vows. You said, "For better or worse, richer or poorer." The question is did you take that part of your vows seriously? The vows are not just something we say because of tradition. They are words that we speak but they are also commitments that we are making. In that ceremony we pledge our lives to another person until death. That means something!

Another reason for divorce I hear from couples is "We grew apart" or "We fell out of love." What is that? Basically what you're saying is I don't like you anymore. There are definitely times when I don't like my wife and there are times when my wife does not like me. But guess what? Feelings change like the wind and as much as you don't like that person right now, give it two weeks and you'll find something to like about them again. It's a matter of your feelings and if you allow your life to be governed by your whims you'll be in for a rollercoaster ride for the rest of your life. Instead of staying steady you are being guided by these reckless emotions. I choose to remain steady regardless of how I feel at the time and that's another reason why divorce is not an option for me. There are times my wife and I don't get along and we disagree so bad to where we can't be in the same room, but it's about working through that. That's what marriage is all about and when you have those types of disagreements and you're able to work through it, then you begin to walk out the true calling of marriage. The human side, the fleshy side says "I don't like you or I don't like your ways" but then you begin to put your flesh aside and work according to the Spirit and then you're able to work it out. You're able to see past the minute issue and see the bigger picture.

$$\mathscr{D} \quad \mathscr{D} \quad \mathscr{D}$$

I actually went down to the courthouse to inquire about a divorce and a random lady pulled me out of line to ask me how she could help (nobody but God intervening). I was hurting because I felt my husband had emotionally abandoned me. Well, my husband moved out and eventually I moved in with my Father with my two kids and I was preggars. During that time I began to pray even more and press into what God was desiring for us. God unequivocally spoke that He would reconcile us and divorce never was in His plan. I had to learn to wait on the Lord to move on my husband's heart and strengthen me to trust and love the at times unlovable. I began confessing over our marriage every morning and continued to serve others throughout the separation as God grew my faith life. That's when change happened and my husband called me to initiate marriage counseling. The counselor was also a christian minister and the Holy Spirit gave him wisdom to get both of us to a breaking point where we humbled ourselves and forgive.

KENNETH AND ANGELA LEWIS,
MARRIED AUGUST 13, 2005

Divorce was never in God's plan and therefore it should not be an option. One of the issues that God deals with us on through marriage is selfishness. Nothing shows you how selfish you are as a person like marriage. It's not about you anymore. It's about us. It's no longer "What do I want to do today?" It's "What should we do today?" If anybody is going to call you out on your selfishness it's going to be your spouse and it's up to you to overcome that. When you overcome that selfishness you are becoming more and more like God. You are never going to be perfect on this Earth however, I believe that this Earth is a training ground and we are to continue to perfect ourselves and perfect that image that God is.

Divorce is not the plan of God because it separates the family and this too was not His plan. In **Genesis 1:27-28** we see that God created male and female, establishing the marriage unit, then He said to them be fruitful and multiply; establishing His plan for the family unit. We have kids who look up to this godly figure that is mom and dad united and they learn from that example. When you separate, they no longer have that example to draw from. Now all they see is hurt and resentment. I even saw it with my own family. For instance, I have three sisters whom I love dearly. However, two of my sisters did not grow up in the same house as me, as they are from my dad's first marriage. Consequently, I was never really given the opportunity to build a true sibling relationship with them. The dismantling of my dad's first marriage pretty much prevented us from bonding and it doesn't feel good. I wasn't even the one whose parents actually divorced so I can't imagine what my sisters went through. No one wins in divorce. When you break up the unit of marriage you only get half of the deal and the effect it has on children can be damaging. Research proves that children from single parent homes, specifically under the circumstance of divorce experience more emotional and behavioral problems than children whose parents are married.[2] Specifically, some short-term effects include social adjustment, academic performance and emotional well-being whereas long-term effects include dealing with anger and aggression, gender identity and separation problems due to the absence

---

2   Cherlin, A. J., Furstenberg,Frank F.,,Jr, & al, e. (1991). Longitudinal studies of effects of divorce on children in great britain and the united states. *Science*, 252(5011), 1386.

of a parent.[3] The effects are even more harmful should one parent be absent from the child's life. Our children need us to be committed to loving one another because the love they see from us affects their well being now and has an enormous affect on their future.

Marriage is not easy, but neither is divorce. It's not just signing a piece of paper and going off to being happy; skipping down the yellow brick road. There's turmoil, there's pain and sometimes divorce brings out the worse in people. Some spouses aren't cooperative and refuse to move forward. Every guy I've ever met who has been divorced has said that they regretted it. They said they wish they had worked it out. Count the cost. Don't be so quick to yell out the D-word. In fact, make it a practice not to use that word at all. Focus on the love, focus on the commitment. Look at the unconditional example of the love that Christ has set for us and apply that to your relationship daily.

---

3   Kalter, N. (1987). Long-term effects of divorce on children: A developmental vulnerability model. *American Journal of Orthopsychiatry, 57*(4), 587-600.

THE VOW

I vow to no longer let divorce be an option for me. The D-word is now forbidden from my thoughts and my speech. I vow to hold true to my commitment of "for better or worse" and make love my first response. When it's hard, when it's tough, when I want to leave, when I want to give up, I will instead faithfully and firmly stay devoted to my spouse demonstrating the unconditional love of God.

Unpack
By Arian T. Moore

You've packed your bags in your mind,
Already you've left the love behind.
Unpack your bags.
You've given up on the love you used to hold dear.
You've given in to the hurt and caved in to the fear.
Unpack your bags.
There's hope, unpack
Have faith, unpack
Make good on your promise to love…
Unpack.

BIBLE STUDY 2

GRACE

As Christians, we are taught that we are saved by grace but what does that mean? Grace is referred to as unmerited favor; or immunity. It is a pardon for all of our past, present, and future sins given to those that believe in Jesus Christ. This grace is given to us, not because of anything that we have done or can do, but because of what Jesus did on the cross. Because of the sacrifice Christ made we are no longer condemned and God's mercies are new every morning. In other words, even though we deserve judgment, God's grace covers us. Because we are saved, we are immune.

While this way of thinking can most certainly be applied to any relationship, I wholeheartedly believe marriage is where grace is needed most. I am commissioned to love my wife in the same way Christ loves His church. So since we are to love like Christ, we must first understand that this is an impossible feat without grace. Despite our spouse's flaws or inadequacies, we give them grace, because we have made a decision to love them no matter what.

Does God's grace give us the right to live in sin? No. We are called to live by the spirit, not the flesh (our sinful nature). To this end, your spouse is not given a pass to mistreat you or be inconsiderate of your feelings with the knowledge that grace is a factor. On the contrary, this grace should motivate them to be loyal all the more.

The fact that my wife didn't leave me when I surely deserved to be left only motivated me to do the right thing. It was her unconditional love that made me feel like an idiot for doing what I did. For that reason, I vowed to never hurt her like that again. Likewise, when we are able to grasp even a general concept of just how much God loves us—in our unfaithfulness He remains faithful—we instantly develop a stronger desire within ourselves to turn away from sin while simultaneously turning to God. So just as God's grace is what brings us to true repentance, the grace extended to your spouse is what is going to lead him or her to a change of heart.

SCRIPTURAL REFERENCES:

Therefore, there is now no condemnation for those who are in Christ Jesus, because through Christ Jesus the law of the Spirit who gives life has set you free from the law of sin and death. For what the law was powerless to do because it was weakened by the flesh, God did by sending his own Son in the likeness of sinful flesh to be a sin offering. – **Romans 8:1-3**

In him we have redemption through his blood, the forgiveness of sins, in accordance with the riches of God's grace. – **Ephesians 1:7**

What shall we say, then? Shall we go on sinning so that grace may increase? By no means! We are those who have died to sin; how can we live in it any longer? – **Romans 6:1-2**

But Jesus said, "Not everyone is mature enough to live a married life. It requires a certain aptitude and grace. – **Matthew 19:11 MSG**

DISCUSSION QUESTIONS:

1. (Singles) How does this revelation of grace change your perception of Christ's love for us?
2. (Married Couples) What are some ways you can institute the grace element into your relationship?
3. (Married Couples) Are there specific areas where you need grace from your spouse?

CHAPTER FOUR

Seasons

Hers

I love when the seasons change from summer to fall. It's my absolute favorite time of the year; crisp air, leaves falling and the smell of pumpkin in the air. Most of us welcome the change of seasons in respect to weather but what about the changing seasons in our marriage? **Ecclesiastes 3:1** says, *"To everything there is a season, and a time to every purpose under the heaven."* There will be sunny days but there will also be storms and maybe even hurricanes within the span of a marriage. The staying power of a marriage depends on a couple's ability to survive the change of seasons.

By year four of our marriage I remember wishing things were like they used to be when we first started dating. I missed the constant catering to and the spontaneous dates. Eventually, I realized that we were in a new season and that instead of looking back on the past in want, I should embrace the season I was in, making the most of every moment.

FUNNY FINANCES

There have been many season changes in our time together. Year three proved to be a tumultuous season for us. We lost everything, a baby (miscarriage), a car, a house and we nearly lost our faith. It is a time in our life that I will never forget. At the time, it just seemed like we were under attack from every angle. My grandmother passed away and we had to borrow money just to make it to her memorial. We were going to church pantries for food and we were desperately selling items just to get buy. I vividly remember taking a bag of clothes to a consignment shop expecting to get at least $30. They took about four items out of the entire stuffed bag. Deflated is the only word I could use to describe the way I felt when the lady handed me seven dollars. We had no gas; only enough to get back home and we needed food. We drove home and walked to the store with that seven dollars to get groceries.

The devastation of our financial situation added pressure to the marriage relationship. There were more arguments than usual and we just couldn't get along. This is why finances are deemed as one of the number one causes of divorce; because it unsettles the marriage. Men are wired to provide so not being able to stresses them out, on the other hand, the woman craves and desires security, not being secure stresses her out. The added stress individually leads to stress in the relationship. The result is often arguments and disagreements, blaming one another for the current situation and even questioning your spouse's ability to contribute to the household.

If the money is tight or you are flat out broke like we were, find free things to do that bring you two closer. M.L. and I would go for this long walk downtown. We would walk through Atlanta's Centennial Olympic Park, down Peachtree Street then back down North Avenue and pass the famous Varsity restaurant. During those times we had so much fun just talking to one another and those memories are priceless.

It's not easy but you can make it through financial problems. A foundation of faith is what helped us and I encourage any couple experiencing financial issues to seek God (read **Jeremiah 29: 13**).

FAMILY PROBLEMS

We almost didn't make it after that first year but thank God we grew up & decided to grow together. Quick things I've learned:

- Shut up. Yup. We both shut up a lot with each other. There's no point in arguing because we aren't divorcing. Choose your battles. We pursue peace like crazy in our home, put on our big girl and boy pants and act like Christian adults and yes, we are really actually happy.
- Protect your marriage. My husband and I are one flesh and I want to make sure others see him like they see me. I will always be his number one fan & vice versa. I ain't sharing our arguments with people who will hold onto it long after we made up.
- We don't bring up the past. It's behind us for a reason. Move on.
- If your spouse is saying a concern, listen. They know you best and believe them.
- You better learn to be content broke or with money because that can make or break your marriage. You better believe if we ever got evicted, we would be evicted together in a tent on the street.

- HEATHER LINDSEY
(CORNELIUS LINDSEY)
MARRIED AUGUST 14, 2010

There may be seasons of distrust after hurt or seasons of family discord. We have been through both and these were hard seasons. After marriage, it took a while for me and my new family (in-laws) to get a feel for each other. My husband had some mama's boy qualities that made bonding with my mother-in-law quiet difficult. Couple that with the fact that my in-laws live in another state; needless to say bonding was difficult. We had some very major arguments and it seemed like we would never see eye to eye, especially after my children were born. There were certain things I wanted in place that were foreign to them and my parents alike. There was also trouble with my side of the family and family members questioning the way M.L. and I ran our household. This too can weigh heavy on a marriage. When there are family problems, couples can get in the habit of sharing too much which does no good at all. We learned to never share our marital problems with our parents under any circumstance. Parents will generally take sides and draw conclusions based on limited knowledge. We are even selective about sharing information with friends. Having a mediator is definitely a good thing but its best to find neutral ground; someone who won't pick sides. Safe guarding your marriage and being on the same page no matter what is pivotal to making it through this season. Remember you are married to your spouse, not your mom, not your dad and not the family.

Having children may also cause conflict in the relationship. Why? Because you are both from two different households and may have different ideals about how to raise children. Will we co-sleep? Will we spank? Will we do public or private school? These decisions can feel like roadblocks if the two of you have a different perspective based on how you were raised. My suggestion here is to be open and flexible. I will not have you to believe that we have not had a number of disagreements over topics like these, but remember a disagreement helps us to arrive at a compromise. Don't aim to do things the way your parents did them. That may not work for your family and the idea here is to find what works for your family. The goal is to create a loving, God fearing home where the children are safe and healthy. And because all children are different there is no one way to approach that. Ask God for wisdom and guidance in helping the both of you make decisions and set family rules and goals.

It should also be noted that just because you talk about these things before marriage, your spouse may change when the children come. For example, when we married my idea was to be a working mom. In fact,

I had accepted a job offer while pregnant with my first son. But after I held that baby and bonded with him, I was convinced that God would help us find a way for me to work from home.

SEX AND DATES

Sex is another issue that is often blamed for couples running to the court house for a divorce. If the expectation is to be swinging from chandeliers from the honeymoon until the end of time there will surely be disappointment. We entered a new season of our love life after having children. It's like playing double dutch sometimes trying to have sexual intimacy with three children, especially when they are small and dependent. As a nursing mom my desire simply faded and the thought of physical intimacy was far from my mind. From a woman's perspective all I can say to the women in that situation is to be willing. To the husband, I can only recommend that you empathize with what your wife is going through and understand the miracle that she has given you (a new life).

While you may be in the season of parenting small children, make time to connect physically and become masters of quickies. No you may not be able to carry on like you did before, but connecting in those few moments is just as significant. I had a personal trainer say to me "its quality, not quantity that matters." Be willing when the opportunity presents itself. Apply this same principle to the love making. Overall, your mindset determines your success at anything in life and this is no different in marriage. If you want a positive outcome, you have to approach the situation with a positive attitude.

Not only did the physical aspect become frustrating but also the relational aspect. We spent four years as a couple before we had children so we became accustomed to dates every weekend and coming and going as we desired. Needless to say, this changed once we had children. Dates are now once a month but they are so precious and necessary. But again, this is a season, it won't last always. The key is to embrace and appreciate the season you are in and make the very best of it.

'TUDES AND TALKS

Attitude…now that changes too. I was much meaner when I first met my husband than I am today. The baggage from my childhood and past hurts caused me to build so many walls. My husband has also changed his attitude in a number of areas, mostly for the better but this can become frustrating when you become accustomed to dealing with certain personality traits. Think of marriage like a football game. Every quarter, the team has to make adjustments to stay competitive in the game. There may be injuries or surprise plays, but no matter what; the team has to quickly realign to win. The same is true in marriage. The person you married won't be the same or think the same twenty years from now. Why? Because we are all changing, learning and growing every day. Certain principles that I once felt strongly about, I no longer feel the same way about. Give your spouse room to grow and don't stifle their growth by forcing them into becoming stagnant. Only the Creator is unchanging, but to be more like Him we have to be constantly changing and transforming our minds.

Change is an inevitable part of life and marriage. For example, the communication may change depending on the season or circumstance. Your husband might be more agitated because bills are past due so he might be short with you or your wife may be feisty because she is hormonal after having a baby or going through menopause. That's not to say that being mean or rude is acceptable but it should be known that we will all have moments where we need grace. Arguments will happen in any marriage. No marriage is free from a disagreement but its understanding that disagreeing is one way in which we find our way to the next level. We disagree to find a compromise and those compromises help us work as a team.

What we have to realize is that the finances are not the issue, the sex is not the issue, neither are the family problems. In the lifespan of a marriage, we should expect that there will be times of surplus and maybe times of drought, but this is covered in the vows we made. We should expect family problems and changes in personalities. These things are just a part of life and going through them does not mean that there is something wrong with your marriage. Even the vows reflect the fact that there will be seasons saying, "In sickness and in health, for better or worse, for richer or poorer…" Regardless of our circumstance, our commitment to stand is unwavering. We have to realize that the season we are in now is only for a time, the season WILL change. Storms don't last always.

His

One of the greatest culture shocks in marriage is the different seasons that you experience. You get married and you're in the honeymoon phase where everything is wonderful, you can't keep your hands off each other; you can't seem to stop saying I love you. That season does not last forever; in fact it may come and go. Something may interrupt that season, be it a financial situation or the entrance of children. These things change the dynamics of a relationship. With children it's no more going to and fro as you please, now you have to consider getting children ready, packing diaper bags and sippy cups. When you have children you have to understand that there are some things you just can't do in this season. For example, before kids my wife and I used to go out all the time, every night had the potential to be a date night. We would peruse the Internet searching for new restaurants to try. When our first child was born, we would try to continue with our random dates only to find that the baby would just cry or bang on the table with the spoon. The fact is we shouldn't have been going to fancy restaurants with a baby. Instead, we learned to find kid-friendly restaurants because that's the season we are in. You see this all the time with new parents bringing their babies to the movie theater and then they get upset with the baby for crying during the whole movie. Crying is what babies do and the better, more appropriate realization is that a movie theater is just not the place for a baby. Desperate for a date night? Find a sitter or someone that can watch the baby while you and your spouse enjoy one another. We started having date nights at least once a month. It allows us to reconnect with one another and it's not always going out to eat, sometimes we just go for a walk together. If going out is not an option, find a way to have some time alone when the children are asleep. Watch a movie, take a bubble bath, watch the game together; do whatever the two of you love. It's the quality of the time spent, not necessarily what you are doing. Being able to appreciate whatev-

Yes, having children has changed the dynamic of our relationship in this season. It becomes more difficult to go on dates as we used to. We can't just take off for the weekend or splurge on gifts for one another. We know that this is but a season of our lives together. Our children will grow and become independent and as they do, we will slowly regain some of the time back that it takes to invest in them at this stage.

We believe that our romantic relationship is only one dimension of the life we live together. There is a friendship and a partnership in all things – including raising our children and we take pleasure in the fact that we get to do that together. So we try to appreciate the moment. When one of us is frustrated, the other engages their capacity to be patient with the children. We use a lot of laughter to get us through the long nights!

Ultimately we count it a privilege to have children in the first place. So for now, we have family dates. We hang out together. And when the babies sleep, mommy and daddy take a moment to reconnect – even if we have to hide in the closet to do it. We have two daughters and a baby on the way at the time of this writing. So clearly, they are not stopping our fun at all!

– *ANDREW AND JULI-ANNE JAMES*,
MARRIED SEPTEMBER 12, 2009

er time you can have together is the mentality you have to have to make it through the changing seasons of marriage.

LACK ATTACK

The season of lack is one that is hard for most marriages. It was especially hard for mine. My wife married me and had a sense of security. I was in the Navy and in school, so she had stability and benefits. When I decided to get out of the Navy things weren't as smooth. I was trying to get my business off the ground while she was working every day. In the beginning the business seemed promising; we were looking at new houses and planning for a very prosperous future. Then all of a sudden it seemed like someone turned the faucet off. I remember my wife coming to me saying, "Do you have any more clients coming in?" "No, but I can go get some," I said. Her response was, "I think maybe you should look for a job." Yet I remained in denial because

> When it comes to dealing with difficult situations in our marriage, we have learned that an open line of communication is important as well as understanding we are each other's best friend and no matter what we go through we go through it together. I remember when we went to the Family Services to apply for WIC and Food stamps. Yes, I said it Food Stamps. We were a young couple with a baby therefore we had to do what we didn't want to do.
>
> Most men would have let their wife go for the assistance alone because of a male ego. Marcus did just the opposite, he was right by my side. He said this was a temporary fix not a cure all. I don't think I could have gone for government assistance without my best friend being right by my side to help ease any embarrassment I felt. I learned early in my marriage who my best friend for life would be.
>
> *MARCUS AND MARY FLEMING,*
> **MARRIED JUNE 22, 1991**

I believed that I could make the business work. Nothing worked. As I tried everything I knew to make it work, nothing did. At this time we loss a car, downgraded to a one bedroom and had to get food baskets from local churches. Times were rough. Lack is not easy but through these times you have to remain faithful to God. Why? Because you are vulnerable and insecure, and it is during these times that the enemy will throw temptation your way. Some woman may come along and stroke your ego or some man may whisper sweet nothings in your ear that your husband hasn't said in years and the next thing you know you're picking up your clothes off some hotel floor. Your commitment to God is going to determine your ability to stay committed to your spouse. That's why it's so important that when we go through storms we draw nearer to God instead of running away from Him.

As we were going through the mess we went through in that particular season, I can say that I was not faithful to God; in fact I was far from Him. I believe that it was my sin that caused us to be in the predicament we were in. We can't live a life of sin and expect God to bless our mess. So it wasn't my faithfulness to God that saved our marriage during that particular season, but I would say it was the faithfulness of my wife. Remember the two of you are now one and God see's you that way.

So let's recant here, we loss everything, left the church we had dedicated our lives to and had a baby on the way, now that was year three of our marriage. But even as we were writing this book we were going through a storm; I lost my job and my father-in-law passed away. There was both grief and financial strain. Most marriages fail after such devastation. Is our marriage any stronger or any different? Not necessarily, but the unique thing that makes our marriage and any marriage last is one word…commitment. It's that simple really. It's a mindset that says no matter what, I'm here. No storm and no pressure can destroy this relationship. Nothing can deter or destroy the commitment that I've made. I made vows and come hell or high water I am going to carry them out. That's the mentality you have to have to last through any season.

Have an expectation that things will change. Obstacles will come. The same way you faced obstacles as a single person, you will face obstacles as a married person. But the joy and the blessing of marriage is now you have someone to go through those things with you. You have a live-in best friend to lean on, pray with and seek advice from. The bottom line is, life has its ups and downs but we keep living; marriage has ups and downs too and guess what? We stay married.

THE VOW

I know that our marriage relationship will have tests and trials. I know that we won't be the same and that our situations won't always be the same. I am committed to being hopeful during those times. I am committed to seeing the promise during those times. I know that there's something better for us on the other side of a hard time. I vow to love, support and comfort my spouse through whatever storm we experience and to be open to making our love last through any season no matter how uncomfortable or difficult.

Weather

By Arian T. Moore

Grabbed my umbrella
It started to rain
Pit
Pat
Pit
Pat.
The rain kept falling.
I held his hand tighter.
The rain kept falling.
Pit
Pat
Pit
Pat
The rain came harder
Then thunder.
Boom
The storm.
The darkness
The rain.
Pit
Pat
Pit
Pat
Sun.

CHAPTER FIVE

Tackling Temptation

Hers

The assumption is that women are not tempted as often as men but that is further from the truth. Perhaps from a physical perspective we aren't as blinded by the thrill of another man, but emotionally we may be. Vulnerabilities leave us all open for the enemy to present opportunities. Whether or not we give in to those opportunities is another story.

I have never physically committed adultery and to be honest I never thought about it. I have however, become emotionally invested in a situation when I, as I stated above, was vulnerable and left myself open. Vulnerable and hurt. That's where I was. My husband and I were just not getting along and our connection

> If you are erasing texts before your spouse can see them, you have already gone too far.
>
> If you are having conversations at work that you would not want your spouse to over hear, you have already gone too far.
>
> If your eyes are lingering over someone's body, you have already committed adultery with them. Your eyes are for your spouse only and they should bounce, not roam, when out in the world.
>
> There should be no secrets in marriage. No accounts that aren't shared, or passwords known.
>
> *- DALE AND TONYA FERGUSON, MARRIED MAY 24, 1990* **(SURVIVORS OF INFIDELITY)**

was just not there. We were arguing, he was mean and I was tired. Emotionally, I was on a roller coaster (and a week or so later I found out why…I was pregnant). But at that moment all I knew was that I felt underappreciated and overlooked. I connected with an old friend on social media and he and I began to chat and next thing I know I was planning to meet this guy for coffee. What? Yes you read right. I was out of my mind. But see how easy it was for me to get to that place. Did I meet with him? No and we both realized how stupid we were being because we both have families and nothing good could come of the situation. Hence, all communication ended.

My husband had a similar situation on social media. Where a woman he worked with in the past had messaged him and they ended up having a long conversation and she invited him out for lunch. He says he had no intention to be inappropriate with her but after rereading the messages he saw where her intent was. So let's just lay down some ground rules for social media and Internet behavior for married people:

1. You should not be social media friends with old flames or people that you are highly attracted to.
2. You should avoid exchanging inappropriate messages with people of the opposite sex.

These rules apply to social media as well as email and text messaging or even physical, one-on-one exchanges (For example: you run into an old friend at the mall). To some, these rules may seem extreme but what is your marriage worth to you? Is it worth it? All the enemy needs is an open door, a small window of opportunity and the next thing you know you're meeting your high school crush at the hotel.

I hear so many people say, "What you won't do for your spouse someone else will?" Does that justify us going elsewhere with our hearts or our bodies? No. I am responsible for me and what I do with my body and you are responsible for you. What your spouse does has nothing to do with how you carry yourself as a man or woman of God. Yes my husband was being very ugly towards me at the time but that does not mean that I go out and seek the attention of another man. Instead, I should have fervently prayed for my husband. We can't approach our marriages the same way the world does. In our world, prayer is our defense mechanism.

Prayer and closeness with God allows us to be lead by the spirit so that we are able to stand against temptation. We can see the enemy coming before he even gets a foothold. It is only when we are guided by our emotions (the flesh) that we find ourselves falling into sin and selfishness. We are also more apt to see the way of escape when we are prayerful and close to God. **1 Corinthians 10:13** says *"No temptation has overtaken you except what is common to mankind. And God is faithful; he will not let you be tempted beyond what you can bear. But when you are tempted, he will also provide a way out so*

> In our nearly 23 years of marriage my wife and I have learned we can not avoid temptation, so instead of regularly falling victim to it, we've decided to prepare for it. Victory over temptation in our home comes as we proactively identify the tempters in our lives and we do our best to eliminate them. We live our lives open to one another and allow nothing to be made exclusive to one without the other having full access, including our text messages, internet history, social media accounts, etc.. We've found safety in proactively identifying our tempter and allowing full access to one another. By the grace of God this has allowed us to win more often than lose.
>
> **DARRYL MORRISON (JO ANN MORRISON), MARRIED MAY 29, 1993**

that you can endure it." Though He provides a means of escape we still have to take the way out. There is still the choice. God never makes us do anything; He always gives us the choice to do His will. I remember being a single woman and while on my way to sin I would hear God say, "Turn around, go back home," yet I kept driving. Instead of taking the way of escape, I chose to do what I wanted to do. God gives us the tools that we need to remain loyal and faithful, but there are actions that we have to take as well.

On the other hand, some may be in a situation where infidelity has occurred. A girlfriend of mine recently learned of her husband's unfaithfulness and despite her anger and hurt, she was willing to work it out. I asked her what compelled her to hold on to her marriage, she said, "Because he's my friend first and I love him." Any couple experiencing this should seek God on how to move forward. God can heal any situation and many marriages overcome. It will take willingness, time and counseling, but restoration is possible.

His

The one impression I absolutely do not want you to take away from this book, above all other misconceptions, is that I am the perfect husband that has never experienced temptation of any kind. I would hate for you to get the sense that I walk around with specially made blinders over my eyes to prevent me from seeing attractive and beautiful women on a daily basis. As much as I wish every woman that is not my wife was downright ugly to me, that is just not the case. I also don't want you to look at me as one who has never experienced the flirting or bold invitations of quite a few females from time to time. So, how do I

We conducted an anonymous social media survey and asked couples to discuss infidelity; whether they had survived it and what parameters they have set in place to prevent it from happening again. Here are the results:

- Respondents had been married for 8 to 12 years.
- Respondents identified that their highest point of temptation was from old friends.
- For those who experienced infidelity and decided to work it out they explained that they were much closer than they were before.
- The answers given for ways to prevent infidelity again was developing trust, communication and counseling.

deal with the bombardment of temptation that is virtually everywhere? Truthfully the answer can be found in one word, boundaries.

I developed the understanding of the need for boundaries after struggling with an addiction to pornography for many years. I saw my first porno magazine at the age of seven years old, and by the time I turned eight I had seen more X-rated movies than I can remember. This exposure created a lust and thirst for other women that affected me well into my marriage. While I never physically cheated on my wife with another woman, I've been involved in numerous adulterous affairs in my mind with porn as the means of entry. Jesus warned, *"But I tell you that anyone who looks at a woman lustfully has already committed adultery with her in his heart"* (**Matthew 5:28**). It's not like I was watching pornography because of the great acting, I was watching it for the purpose of lustful self-gratification; therefore I stood guilty as charged. I understood that I had a problem and I needed to change, especially because this ordeal caused my wife a lot of hurt and affected her level of trust. After dedicating my life to Christ in my mid-twenties and coming into the understanding that watching porn did not please God, I started praying that God would deliver me from that addiction. What I ultimately discovered was that "faith without works is dead;" my faith required a corresponding action. After falling over and over again, it was evident that I needed to create some boundaries if I sincerely desired God's deliverance. (Read more in the book The Godly vs. Sexy: From Porn to Purpose by M.L. Moore).

Boundaries are necessary for success in any area of life. Without boundaries we are left unguarded and wide open for the enemy to come in and wreak havoc; this is especially the case in marriage. To put it plainly, where there are no boundaries there is always an invitation for the enemy to divide and conquer. So do whatever you have to do to make it extremely difficult for you to yield to temptation.

While porn was my biggest issue, it was not the only instance where boundaries were necessary in my marriage. There was this woman, a nice looking woman, who kept coming to speak to me just about every day at work. I mean she came day after day, flirting and smiling. In my mind, I'm like "Lord why does this lady keep coming over here." Despite the fact that I talked to her about my wife and repeatedly told her how much I was in love with my wife, she wasn't bothered at all. It became obvious what she wanted when she said, "I wish I had a man like you." And that's when I had to nip the situation in the bud. I let her know that it wasn't going down and that I wasn't interested in ever being with any woman other than my wife. She never spoke to me again after that. Joseph did the same thing when Potiphar's wife tempt-

> I had to learn about the importance of boundaries after living a life influenced by pornography and promiscuity. I wanted to make sure that I was going to totally commit myself to my wife. The guys that talked about women all the time and sex with those women, I had to stop hanging around. I stopped listening to music that talked about sex such as hardcore rap and I stopped watching movies with nudity and hardcore sex scenes. I was willing and still am willing to do whatever it takes to guard my heart and keep my mind focused on God and my goal of continuing to be faithful to my wife.
> **NIKKI BONNER (FALON BONNER), MARRIED NOVEMBER 3, 2012**

ed him. Day after day she tried him but one day she had him cornered, Joseph ran.

This isn't an isolated incident. I wear my ring, I post pictures on social media of my wife and me, I even boast about my love for her, yet women still try me. I had to walk out of a pizza parlor because a woman basically let me know that she wanted me with no strings attached. What did I do? I ran right up out of there. It's not worth it. I remember when Dr. Creflo Dollar, speaking in reference to a woman who tried to seduce him at the church, once said something like, "I don't care how fine you are; I don't give a doggone if you got fireworks coming out your butt, I will escort you right out of here." It's really that simple and that serious at the same time. But so I don't have to run, I make an effort not to put myself in situations that require a sprint by creating boundaries.

Some of the boundaries I have in place and recommend are:

🕊 **Clean Media.** Be mindful of what you expose yourself to via media, especially the things you look at. You shouldn't be meditating on, listening to or watching anything that tempts you. Webster's Dictionary describes pornography as the presentation of sexually explicit behavior, as in a photograph, intended to arouse sexual excitement. This means not only are porn videos porn, but so are some social media images and TV series scenes. And maybe porn is not your issue, maybe its saying no to the flirtatious advances of the opposite sex. Watching TV shows that condone adulterous behavior could very well be a stumbling block for you. **Philippians 4:8** says, *"Finally, brothers and sisters, whatever is true, whatever is noble, whatever is right, whatever is pure, whatever is lovely, whatever is admirable—if anything is excellent or praiseworthy—think about such things."* Remember that what you watch and listen to is ultimately a seed that you are sowing in your heart. Make sure that you are sowing good seeds so that good things spring up.

"Above all else, guard your heart, for everything you do flows from it" (**Proverbs 4:23**).

🕊 **Start with the Check in**. You should check in with your spouse.

🕊 **Disclose Passwords.** Your passwords should be disclosed so that you leave no room for temptation. Your spouse should have access to your social media accounts.

🕊 **Get a New Crew.** Watch who you hang around. We are all influenced by the company we keep. **1 Corinthians 15:33** says, *"Do not be misled: "Bad company corrupts good character."* Personally, I limit my relationships with other guys simply because of this issue. I'm not going to hang around some guys that are okay with cheating on their wives. It's not worth it! It is always easier to influence the good to do bad than it is to convince the bad to do good.

🕊 **Pray and Stay in His Word.** *"Keep watch and pray, so that you will not give in to temptation. For the spirit is willing, but the body is weak!"* (**Matthew 26: 41**). This is a spiritual battle and we have to fight in the spirit. Will power is not enough, we need the Holy Spirit. Your prayer life and your relationship with God is essential. Pray every day and cover yourself in God's word—the Bible.

🕊 **The Lust of the Eyes.** Stop looking at the opposite sex lustfully. Trust me, I used to do this all the time because lets be real, women are beautiful. But there's something more that happens when we look. The phrase "Nothing's wrong with looking" is a great lie, simply because "looking" is where lust of any kind begins—especially sexual lust. Jesus said *"You have heard that it was said, 'Do not commit adultery.' But I tell you that any man who looks at a woman lustfully has already committed adultery with her in his heart* (**Matthew 5:27-28**)." Every sexually lustful desire begins with a look or a peep, followed by a lustful thought, which leads to lustfully driven actions. Through our eyes and imagination Satan sexually tempts us by placing opportunities of fulfillment in our line of sight. When we see the opportunity, his mission then is to invade our thought process with the intentions of leading us closer towards a lustfully driven decision, which then yields a physical reaction that is also motivated by lust. "There's nothing wrong with looking" is a complete contradiction to what Jesus said. In fact, in this scripture Jesus makes it extremely clear that your eyes are very capable of causing you to sin. In **Luke 11:34** Jesus tells us, *"Your eye is the lamp of your body. When your eyes are good, your whole body also is full of light (goodness). But when they are bad, your whole body is full of darkness (evil)."* You might have to turn your head at the mall (I do) and delete some social media friends who dress provocatively (I do). Your marriage and your family are totally worth that sacrifice.

THE VOW

I vow to keep my eyes on my spouse. I will not look to the left or to the right. I will be faithful and loyal to my spouse. I will set boundaries so that I am not tempted to destroy the covenant that I have made. My marriage means more to me than a good time. My spouse means more to me than my ego. I will not let my family down. I will trust God to always provide a way of escape, but more importantly I will always take the way out.

Feels Good

By Arian T. Moore

Looks good on the outside,
But inside she's a bag of condemnation.
Smooth and sensual on the outside,
But inside he's laden with shame.
A moment seems good,
A moment feels right,
But the result is destruction.
What feels good for a moment results in...
Death.
Buried is the trust,
Lifeless is the marriage,
Destroyed are the vows.
Can't take it back,
The pain lives on,
Don't look outside,
Turn to the one you love.

CHAPTER SIX
Me, Myself and I

Hers

Because we are so accustomed to doing things a certain way, we can selfishly expect our spouse's to do things the way we expect them done. I remember my husband complaining about finding his socks still raveled in the dryer. He said, "How many times do I have to tell you to unravel the socks? If you don't unravel the socks they don't get clean." I don't remember where that went but I'm pretty sure it went south and I probably told him to unravel his own socks. Some may be asking, "How is that selfish?" Well, it's selfish because he wasn't considering the fact that I washed his clothes, instead he focused on the fact that he wanted his laundry done a certain way. Here's the fool proof test, ask yourself, is this about me and my desires or my spouse's desires? If it's about you then, ding ding ding!!! That's being selfish.

The dictionary defines selfishness as concerned primarily with one's own interests, benefits, welfare, etc., regardless of others. In other words, when it's all about you, I can guarantee you that you are operating in selfishness. Having children, I've learned that we are naturally selfish and we don't consider the feelings of others by nature. Think about a baby; that baby doesn't care if you are tired, he is going to cry and cry until you get up and change him or get him some milk. The same is true when children get older, they want what they want when they want it and they generally could care less about how it inconveniences you. We have to learn to be unselfish and to care for others. It's something that we have to train ourselves to do and it often comes through practice and by renewing our minds. And we renew our minds though the word of God.

Jesus is our role model; our example of how we should live and He gave such an awesome example of unselfishness. Some key scriptures here are:

Philippians 2:3 (NLT) *Don't be selfish; don't try to impress others. Be humble, thinking of others as better than yourselves.*

1 John 15:12-13 (NLT) *This is my commandment: Love each other in the same way I have loved you. There is no greater love than to lay down one's life for one's friends.*

Wow! What a revelation! We are called to lay our lives down for our spouse's. Laying down our life means that we put aside our wants to give the other person the advantage. We consider our spouse before we consider ourselves.

Romans 12:10 (NLT) *Be devoted to one another in love. Honor one another above yourselves.*

James 3:15-16 (NLT) *For jealousy and selfishness are not God's kind of wisdom. Such things are earthly, unspiritual, and demonic. For wherever there is jealousy and selfish ambition, there you will find disorder and evil of every kind.*

Let's pause right there. That scripture basically said that where there is selfishness, there is disorder. There is chaos, mayhem and confusion in a house where selfishness has taken root. Instead, we are to value our spouse's interest above our own interest. In other words we are called to **SERVE**. When you have a mindset of service, you don't focus so much on me, my and mine. Service is the opposite of selfishness because you are intentionally supplying the needs of someone else. It is also a demonstration of love to serve others. *"For even the Son of Man came not to be served but to serve others and to give his life as a ransom for many"* (**Mark 10:45 NLT**). Serving means that you are willfully catering to the needs, wants and desires of another person. Instead of serving myself all the time, I am consciously serving my spouse daily. How do I do this? Well that's going to look different for every marriage relationship. For me, I cook dinner for my husband every day. I've done that since we first married

> Some examples of selfishness in our marriage were Brandon not understanding that by helping Samantha clean more it left her with more energy for other "activities" and Samantha being too busy with business and work to realize it used up much of her time and there was little left for home (cooking, romance, etc). These are areas in which we were not thinking about the other person and what we learned is that part of marriage is about being subservient to your partner. It's about compromising and letting go of a me, my, mine, my way mentality. It becomes US. And if you are selfish about anything in your marriage, it's no longer "us." The other person will somehow get shorted because you chose not to consider or think of them and their feelings. And we all know what can happen when a person feels shorted. They tend to gravitate towards something or someone else to feel their void and get what they need. We have to stand together in OUR marriage.
>
> *BRANDON AND SAMANTHA ROBBINS,* **MARRIED DECEMBER 20, 2014**

and it brings me joy to serve him in that way. He has never asked for that, but it's something that I enjoy doing as a demonstration of my love for him. I also fix his lunches for work every day, again that's something that I enjoy. Find out what your spouse likes and make a conscious decision to serve him or her in that way. My husband likes pizza once a week, so I make that happen. What does your spouse like? Think about what small things you can do to serve your spouse every day; something that you may not like doing, but that you do because it makes your spouse happy. Think about Jesus and the sacrifice that He made by serving us, I'm sure dying on the cross was not His first choice, yet He did it because His heart was to serve. Have a servant's heart for your spouse.

By doing so not only do we strengthen our marriages, but we also set an example of serving others for our children. Though my parents ultimately divorced, I candidly recall the way they served each other and it helped me set the bar for the type of marriage that I wanted. I remember my dad running my mom's bathwater and I remember him washing her hair. I remember my mom fixing my dad's plate and preparing his lunch for work. One of my fondest memories is of them greeting each other with a kiss every day. Children learn by what they see, not what we say and in most cases what they see from our relationship will affect their ideals on marriage and relationships in the future. What example do you want to set? One of selfishness or one of service? I decided that I want to raise children who think of others first and to do that they have to see me exhibit that behavior at home and in the world at large.

Statistics quote finances, communication and sex as the number one, two and three reasons for divorce, but when you are focused on your spouse's needs and not your own these are no longer issues. In every area you are considering your spouse; in your spending and budget setting, in how you communicate with your spouse and how you make love to your spouse. It's about them not about you.

Now when you go about having a mindset of service towards your spouse, do it with a pure heart and not with ulterior motives. It is true that you reap what you sow, but you should never do anything seeking some benefit. You should do it because you genuinely want to serve your

> Yielding! Yielding! Yielding! Daily we have opportunities to disagree, assert our will over one another's and disregard each other's feelings or opinions. Whether in making decisions with our kids or business, we don't always have the same thought process or even perspective. It can easily become a "battle of wills." Yielding to each other in those moments has kept our marriage strong. It's not a competition. We are on the same team so we create a safe space to share our view without fear of being disregarded, criticized or judged. While we may not always see things the same, we love each other and trust God's word in each of us will prevail so that ultimately our family can win.
>
> *JWYANZA AND DAWN NURIDDIN,*
> **MARRIED OCTOBER 13, 2001**

spouse. When you take on a mindset of 'what about me?' you are falling right back into a mindset of selfishness. Remember this is about your spouse not about you. You say you love your spouse, right? Well service is a demonstration of love. Love is an action word. **John 3:16** tells us that God loved the world so He gave His only son. That gift was a demonstration of God's love. When we serve our spouse's we demonstrate the love we have for them. **1 Corinthians 13** of the Message Bible gives a very good description of how we can demonstrate love to our spouse's saying:

"Love never gives up. Love cares more for others than for self. Love doesn't want what it doesn't have.

Love doesn't strut,
Doesn't have a swelled head,
Doesn't force itself on others,
Isn't always "me first,"
Doesn't fly off the handle,
Doesn't keep score of the sins of others,
Doesn't revel when others grovel,
Takes pleasure in the flowering of truth,
Puts up with anything,
Trusts God always,
Always looks for the best,
Never looks back,
But keeps going to the end.
*Love never dies." **1 Corinthians 13 (MSG)***

When you wake up in the morning, decide how you will serve your spouse and do it. If you have to program a reminder in your phone or keep a note in your pocket, make an effort to serve.

THE MIRROR

One of the problems is that we want to mold our spouse's into miniature versions of us. We want them to think like us, act like us and do the things that we do. We want a spouse who will do it our way because our way is the right way. But think about that for a moment. Do you really want that? Who's challenging you to be better if your spouse is just like you? That means that he or she would have the same weaknesses and strengths as you. Think about it this way 1+3=4 but so does 2+2. While the equation is different, they both get to the same exact destination. Often times we want our spouse's to do things the way we do them, but in many cases there is no right or wrong way. As long as the job gets done does it really matter what route you take?

As uncomfortable as it is to be challenged, it is necessary because our spouse's show us who we really are. Your spouse is like a mirror and you see your real reflection through them. I've discovered so many things about myself that I simply do not like because of my husband pointing it out or me just noticing the way I responded to him. Eventually, you have to learn that there is no right or wrong way. You and your spouse are from two different households and were raised totally different. My husband and I have that exact testimony and in the beginning it made things very uncomfortable. He was used to tomatoes being cut a certain way and PB&J sandwiches made without double dipping the unclean peanut butter knife into the jelly and those small things caused arguments in our home. Why? Because we wanted the other person to do it our way. Here's the thing, there's no such thing as my

> Selfishness creates an environment where there is no family vision, but rather two people seeking to fulfill their own agendas. This will keep a marriage stagnate and keeps them growing both individually and as a partnership. Selfishness also produces mistrust. Mistrust opens the door for many destructive behaviors as a way for self-preservation. This includes hiding money, adultery, lying, etc. Selfishness is the gateway for marriage destruction. The key is to become so assured in who you are and that God ultimately has your life in His hands that you are willing to obey God's Word in submitting to your spouse, humbling yourself and operating in a way to uplift each other without fear.
>
> **KENNETH AND ANGELA LEWIS, MARRIED AUGUST 13, 2005**

way anymore. There's our way. You are no longer single, you are married. It's time to take on a marriage mindset.

Single people often take for granted the independence they have being unmarried. Singleness is an opportunity to do what you want when you want to do it. Something as simple as deciding what you want for dinner and not having to consider another person seems minute and trivial, but for a married couple it can yield a disagreement. And we have had plenty of those. I remember we had a major argument at Rooms to Go because he wanted boring, neutral color furniture and I wanted something with a bit more pop. If I was single I would not have had to consider what he wanted at all and I could have gotten the plush sofa that I wanted (though I would have regretted it later). We both were only thinking about what we wanted, not about the other person's desires.

Being married means that I consider my spouse; what matters to him matters to me. It's hard to have this mindset in a society that is selfish to its core but it's the mindset that is required to have a successful marriage. The obstacle we face is the idea that we have to preserve ourselves so we fight against every little thing our spouse brings to us. "Oh no, he is not going to be telling me what to do; I don't know who he thinks he is." "She has lost her mind if she thinks she's going to be running this house." These types of statements are the very things people say who simply want to defend themselves. But the question is what are you protecting yourself from? It took me about nine years of marriage to get this…Your spouse is not the enemy. Your spouse is not out to get you. Your spouse loves you. Your spouse may disagree with you on some things but he/she still loves you and that disagreement does not diminish the sincerity of their love. At the end of the day we had to accept our differences and move on. Come to the realization that your differences are what make you unique and in many cases, your differences are what allow you to complement one another.

𝒮 𝒮 𝒮

At the end of the day we have to stop majoring on the minor things. Only fight for the things that really matter. If your husband wants a Bose system so he can pretend to be at the movie theater, let the man get the Bose. If your wife wants to buy a turquoise loveseat, let her have it. Don't let small things disturb your peace. **James 3:18** says *"And those who are peacemakers will plant seeds of peace and reap a harvest of righteousness."* You can be a peacemaker with the art of compromise. Many people call it compromise with the idea that you both come to a midway point but most times, it's either going to go your way or your spouse's way. I say if it's something that your spouse is passionate about and it doesn't matter as much to you, compromise but if it's something major that you both are passionate about you may want to fast and pray on it and/or get a mediator involved.

Overall, we have to remember that this marriage is an "us" thing not a "me" thing. One of the most unselfish things you can do for your spouse is to pray for them. Pray for their peace. Pray for their health. Pray for their wisdom. Pray the word of God over them and make confessions over their life. Take your spouse to God in prayer, because only God can change the heart of a person, not you. You can talk to your spouse until they are blue in the face and they are still going to do what they want to do and see it their way. Conviction comes from God and through prayer; God can convict your spouse's heart, ultimately producing change. However, those prayers need to be genuine; not asking God to make your spouse see it your way, but rather that God would lead and guide both of you into His perfect will for your lives. Remember if it's all about you and your way, it's selfish.

I want to end with this notion; the act of staying married is in and of itself an act of unselfishness. It's realizing that staying married is not just about you but it impacts your family and even society. Children from two parent households have far greater chances than children from single parent homes, socially, emotionally, academically, etc. But even more importantly, when we stay committed to our spouse's we show the world that love is possible, that marriage can work. We give hope to those married couples who are going through a rough patch. There's nothing like seeing an older couple, holding hands walking down the street after fighting with your spouse. It inspires you and it gives you hope. We have the opportunity to do that for others when we unselfishly declare that we will stick it out. It's not about you!

His

If I can be real honest here, I am naturally a selfish person, so naturally I only think about myself. Nevertheless, I have to consider my wife and that's one of the greatest challenges of marriage for me. I remember my mom telling my wife that she was the best thing that ever happened to me because I was so selfish and she saw some changes in me in that area. As it relates to marriage, it's a constant process of going against this "I want to do what I want to do" mentality. Selfishness has affected me in every area of my marriage, whether it was fixing myself a sandwich and not considering whether or not she had eaten to not washing dishes when I see them piling up or not picking up after myself—all of that is not considering my wife. Selfishness also impacted my marriage as it relates to an addiction to pornography. The addiction caused me to desire to look at porn despite the fact that it would hurt my wife.

Selfishness boils down to a lack of consideration. It's when you consider yourself and no one else. Unfortunately, when you think like that you end up hurting a lot of people. The opposite then is being selfless, and that's when we surrender ourselves to our spouse's. It's saying, "I surrender what I want and my independent habits, and instead we develop new habits together." Have we perfected this? Absolutely not! One area that I still struggle in is football Sundays. On Sundays at 1 o'clock I want to be left alone, I want peace and I want quiet until the game goes off. Now some might argue that that's not a lot to ask. Though this is my struggle, I definitely see the selfishness in the matter. My wife should not have to be on the backburner for a football game. Nothing but God should come before your spouse and if that's not the case, we all need to reevaluate.

SEX

I believe if we take the world's advice on anything we end up at a dead end because the world is selfish. Selfishness is a derivative of this world; it's not from God. There's no selfishness in God so if you're thinking of sex from the perspective of self, "I like this so my spouse needs to do it," then you're not understanding what it means to make love. The Bible says that God is love and there's nothing about God that is selfish so how can you make 'love' to your spouse while thinking about yourself?

> My (the wife) selfish tendencies were exposed to my husband during the first five years of our marriage. I believe it was a byproduct of growing up the youngest of three girls and everyone being concerned about "what I wanted." My husband would "jokingly" refer to my selfish ways and as a result I did not take his "hints" seriously. He of course was concerned about hurting my feelings and did not say to me, "dear you are being selfish when…."
>
> Eventually, we learned that communication was needed to address the selfishness. I assured my husband that I needed him to tell me exactly how he was feeling, even if that meant me becoming emotional. I could not read his mind at this early phase of our marriage. Once my husband felt comfortable with being honest with me even if it seemed a bit "brutal" to me, our communication improved and changes were made in the area of selfishness.
>
> **BERNARD AND EDANA PERRY, MARRIED JULY 6,1985**

Furthermore, I believe that the world has a warped view of sex. It's all about 'me' being satisfied. Where is the love in that? That whole mindset is just selfishness. I believe God created sex for husbands and wives to give of themselves as an expression of love, not for you to get yours and I get mine and we go on about our business. When I make love to my wife now, my goal is to consider her first, not me. Now, this has not always been the case in our marriage. There was a time when I wanted certain things that I had been exposed to via porn or a previous escapade that my wife would often reject because she viewed it as demeaning. Due to my selfish nature I would huff and puff not considering my wife's feelings. I also didn't consider the fact that my mind was perverted. I had to understand that my wife is not my personal pornstar. Therefore, she shouldn't be pressured into doing things that she is uncomfortable with to fulfill my twisted fantasies. In other words, I came to the conclusion that she was not the one with the problem, I was, and I needed help.

It's important for us to understand the reasoning behind God wanting us to wait until marriage to have sex. It is because you can't miss something that you've never had. So if I never had sexual relations with another person then I wouldn't have any ideas about what sex would be like with someone other than my wife. When a husband and wife marry, God's plan is for them to come together as virgins, having nothing sexually to draw from but one another. When you come into the marriage and both people have already had sexual pasts, you now have an idea of what sex should look and feel like and you have developed expectations based on your experiences. Due to the fact that I fell into this category, I had to renew my mind concerning the way in which I viewed sex and my wife. I had to understand that all of the perverted things I learned in my past were from a place of selfishness, not love. I had to understand that sex in marriage is totally different from sex outside of marriage because it gets God's stamp of approval.

I hate to sound super spiritual, but there is an anointing that you experience in a sexual experience that is covered and blessed by God. Two people selflessly giving of themselves to one another is a breathtaking experience like no other. But some married people never get to experience this anointing because they have yet to renew their minds and still bring their past experiences into their marriage. You can't bring your past baggage into your marriage relationship. Ask God to deliver you from past wounds, seek the closure that you need from past relationships and come into the marriage fresh. If you are married and haven't done that, start the process now by renewing your mind with God's word.

RENEWING THE MIND

You renew your mind by getting in the word of God and allowing that word to transform you. **Romans 12:2** says, *"Don't copy the behavior and customs of this world, but let God transform you into a new person by changing the way you think. Then you will learn to know God's will for you, which is good and pleasing and perfect."* As we read the word of God we take on the mentality that we should be a reflection of Christ. **Colossians 3:2** says *"Set your minds on things above, not on earthly things."* Christ was selfless; therefore, we should strive to be selfless. If Christ walked in love, then so should we.

> Remember, in marriage the two are one. Selfishness divides. Luke 11:17 "Every kingdom divided against itself is brought to desolation; and a house divided against a house falleth."
>
> **MICHAEL AND PAMELA CRAIG, MARRIED MAY 17, 1980**

You also have to renew your mind, specifically in the area of sex, by no longer listening to the world and their view of sex whether it's from porn, raunchy books, music or the trendiest Thursday night TV show. These things serve as distractions. When you read God's word you want that word to take root in your heart. In **Matthew 13:3-8** we hear the parable of the sower. It says *"A farmer went out to plant some seeds. As he scattered them across his field, some seeds fell on a footpath, and the birds came and ate them. Other seeds fell on shallow soil with underlying rock. The seeds sprouted quickly because the soil was shallow. But the plants soon wilted under the hot sun, and since they didn't have deep roots, they died. Other seeds fell among thorns that grew up and choked out the tender plants. Still other seeds fell on fertile soil, and they produced a crop..."* You want the word of God to be planted on fertile ground and not be choked by thorns. I know it's a hard concept, but why sow seeds in your heart that don't line up with the type of life you want to live? It's bigger than entertainment; this is your life and your marriage!

So someone asked the question, "Does that mean our sex life has to be boring?" and "Do we have to just do missionary?" Remember that if you both were virgins, nothing would be boring, it all would be a discovery and enjoyable. You have to question why would anything involving me being intimate with my spouse, the love of my life be boring to me? It's only boring because you've had so many experiences and you selfishly want your spouse to do what your previous partners did or some warped fantasy you've come up with based on some porn video. It's not your spouse's fault that you've had those experiences and you shouldn't try to make them do something that they may not feel comfortable with.

Trust me we tackled this issue head on because we both came into the marriage with backgrounds and we had to go through that mind renewal process. It's not a onetime event either. We are constantly in a process of renewing our minds with God's word. Getting into the word will allow you to extract those perverted thoughts about sex and replace them with more pure thoughts. Mind renewal truly comes down to allowing the word of God to change the way you think and the result is a change in behavior.

Men, your wife is your prized possession, she's not some stripper or a night walker. She's your wife so there's a certain level of respect that you should have for her and there's a certain way you treat something that's valuable to you. After struggling with porn, I had to learn this myself. I can't devalue my wife and my love for her by desiring for her to do the things I saw on porn videos. She's my wife and I want our love making to make her feel loved, not trashy. But that mindset requires a mindset of selflessness, a realization that in marriage, my spouse's needs come first.

THE VOW

I vow to be selfless in my marriage. It's no longer about me and what I want; it's about me considering my spouse first. I will make it a daily habit of giving all of myself to my spouse. I will renew my mind in areas where I have allowed traces of my past to seep into my relationship. I will maintain daily Bible reading and prayer and I will be mindful of the seeds that I sow into my heart so that I can protect the ground of my heart. Selflessly I commit myself to making what matters to my spouse matter to me.

Self

By Arian T. Moore

My wife was not my everything,
She was my sometimes.
She was my when I feel like it,
She was my when I'm in the mood.
One day she came to me and said,
"I'm leaving if you don't change your attitude."

So I made her my everything,
She is always in my thoughts,
She is always on my mind,
She is always in my heart.
One day she came to me and said,
"I never want to part."

BIBLE STUDY 3

SELFISHNESS

Selfishness - concerned excessively or exclusively with oneself; seeking or concentrating on one's own advantage, pleasure, or well-being without regard for others.

Being self-focused is the opposite of how we are to behave as men and women of faith, not only in marriage but in our relationships and interactions with others. We are to consider others before ourselves **(Philippians 2:3).**

Some characteristics of a selfish person include the following:

- Their needs come before the needs of others.

- They consider only what is convenient for them.

- They desire to be accommodated in most situations.

- Me is all they can see.

- They are difficult and uncooperative.

- They insist on their way.

Selfishness is the disease that kills marriages. Selfish people are always looking to have the advantage. Being around a selfish person can be draining. They have an excuse as to why they can't do everything, nothing is convenient for them and they expect everyone else's life to stop for them. Instead of living lives that revolve solely around our own interests, we want to operate in unselfishness, meaning that we seek to always give the advantage rather than have the advantage. **1 Corinthians 13** says, "love is not self seeking." Love, the opposite of selfishness, is not thinking, "What about me, what about me, oh Lord what about me."

Love is finding ways to humbly serve others. **Philippians 2:5-11** gives a demonstration of Jesus laying down His life, despite the fact that He was God in the flesh. He didn't look to get His way, force His views on others or have others accommodate His needs. Instead, He became a servant. Develop a servant's heart in your life and marriage by intentionally putting the needs of others first and making what matters to others matter to you.

SCRIPTURE REFERENCES:

Do nothing out of selfish ambition or vain conceit. Rather, in humility value others above yourselves... - **Philippians 2:3**

For where you have envy and selfish ambition, there you find disorder and every evil practice. – **James 3:16**

Turn my heart toward your statutes and not toward selfish gain. – **Psalm 119:36**

DISCUSSION QUESTIONS:

1. (Singles) How can you incorporate this idea of servanthood into your life?

2. (Married Couples) In what areas can you focus more on serving your spouse?

3. (Married Couples) What are some of the ways that your spouse currently serves you? (Thank them for serving you in that way).

CHAPTER SEVEN

Rededication

No matter where you find yourself in your relationship now is the perfect time to rededicate your life to your spouse. Commit yourself to being selfless, keeping God at the center, taking divorce off the table forever, and being willing to adjust to changes. Remember that this marriage relationship is bigger than you two; it's about future generations and the reflection of God's love in the earth.

One way you can start changing the atmosphere in your home and in your marriage is by watching your words. Everything you speak should line up with the word of God. Don't speak negative things over your spouse or marriage. Don't make statements like, "He'll never change" because he won't. Don't make confessions like, "She'll never respect me" because what you speak you will see. It's also important that you not use your words to tear your spouse down but that you use your words to build each other up. **1 Thessalonians 5:11** says *"Therefore encourage one another and build each other up..."* We can build each other up with the word of God and also with complements and words of appreciation. There's trouble brewing when a spouse feels overlooked and underappreciated. Your spouse is faced with enough ridicule out in the world, let home be a place where they are built up. Some examples to use daily are "You look nice today," "Thank you for doing that for me" and "I appreciate all that you do."

It is a biblical truth that there is power in our words. **Proverbs 18:21** says, *"The tongue has the power of life and death, and those who love it will*

> Our marriage works because we focus on what matters. The simplest things are what keep marriages going… We get busy, she cooks for me and we choose peace over chaos.
>
> **BARNEY AND EVE TRADER, MARRIED JANUARY 3, 2006**

eat its fruit." If you want to see change in your spouse, speak change. Tell your spouse, "You are awesome," or "You are the man or woman of God that I need." Speak what you desire to see because the alternative is to speak what you are seeing and then you'll just continue to see that.

You can cultivate this by changing your perspective. If you only focus on your spouse's negative traits it will be hard to find something good to say about them or to them. In fact, you will find yourself complaining to them and criticizing them more often than not. But if you focus on the positive, you can easily find positive things to say. Here's an example, you could complain about the fact that your spouse washed the dishes and then left all the cabinets open or you could be thankful that your spouse washed the dishes. You see how we just found the positive in the situation? There's always a silver lining. Find it and focus on it.

Keep in mind that it won't always be blissful or easy and often times it takes work, but its good work. Marriage changes us for the better when two people are both seeking God's will for their lives. Think about what made you fall in love with your spouse in the first place. Think about the love you once had. Look deep within and see that that person is still there. Work to rediscover that love and that passion by first seeking God and then by doing some practical things to set yourself up for a winning marriage.

Here's the bigger picture...your spouse is not your enemy. We have to realize that there's an all out war against every establishment of Christ, and the most sacred of those is the marriage unit. **John 10:10** makes it clear that the enemy's plan is to steal, kill and destroy. We can't allow the enemy to infiltrate our marriages and we have to recognize who our battle is against to win. He wants to see us give up; his ultimate goal is for us to divorce, thereby affecting an entire future generation of people. But we declare right now that he will not win! We will fight for our marriages! Stop fighting your spouse and start fighting for your spouse using prayer, God's word and the Holy Spirit as your weapons. When we fight with these weapons we are sure to be victorious in our marriages and in our lives as a whole.

PRACTICAL TAKEAWAYS

- Don't start the morning without greeting your spouse.

- Ask your spouse how their day was and listen.

- Don't let the troubles of this world weigh down the marriage.

- Use your words to build your spouse up. Speak and confess the word of God!

- Have a date night at least once a month – it doesn't have to be a fancy date.

- Do something to make your spouse smile every day.

- Pray for your spouse every day.

- When the going gets tough, recognize the enemy and use your weapons (prayer, God's word and the Holy Spirit).

- Laugh and enjoy one another. Don't be so serious.

- Make memories. Life is short and tomorrow is not promised.

COMMITMENT, UNITY, COMMUNICATION, PLANNING

1. COMMITMENT: Marriage is more than a feeling; it's a lifelong commitment. Commitment is revealed in the hard times. Determine to stay committed. Pray for strength and for each other!
2. UNITY: Your spouse isn't the enemy. Problems bring stress. Don't attack each other; instead attack the problem, TOGETHER!
3. COMMUNICATION: Be intentional in your communication. Never talking about what you're going through won't make the problem go away. Be honest with one another. Speak the truth IN LOVE. Create space to talk. It's ok to feel fear but don't allow the fear to control you. Use your words to comfort and encourage each other.
4. PLANNING: Come up with an action plan. What are we going to do? When are we going to do it? Planning ahead can often lessen the stress when the tough times come because you already have a plan on how to deal with it together. This takes commitment, unity, and communication!

PASTOR JAY AND CHRISTY HAIZLIP, MARRIED DECEMBER 27, 1986

We pray that you have been blessed by this book and that it helps put the pieces back together. Our prayer is that you would cleave to your spouse like never before. We love you and we're on this journey with you!

Forever Together,

M.L. Moore & Arian T. Moore

REDEDICATION VOWS

Lord we rededicate our marriage to you right now in the name of Jesus. We declare that you are Lord over our marriage and over our household. We will put your word first and make every decision based on what your word says. We promise to honor one another and to serve one another. We vow to love each other in the same manner that you love us. As we submit our lives to you, we also submit to one another. We vow that no matter what storms come, no matter what we endure, we will stay faithfully committed to one another through sickness, health, prosperity or insufficiency. Our love will go unchanging as your loves does for us.

Remembering My Wedding Day
By: Arian T. Moore

When I woke from my rest,
When I stepped in that dress,
I was prepared to share my life.
When I saw your smile,
When I walked down the aisle,
I looked forward to sharing my life.
When we departed as one,
When all the guests had gone,
We realized our lives had begun.
The celebration and hype,
is all a blur,
yet the vows remain intact.
But what I remember most,
what I will always hold dear,
what I will never forget,
Is…
You.

SALVATION

Perhaps you and your spouse do not know God. Maybe you have yet to experience salvation. Give your life to Jesus today and let the love of Christ transform your heart and your marriage. Say this prayer…

Heavenly Father, your Word says that if I confess with my mouth and believe with my heart that Jesus is Lord, I shall be saved. I believe Jesus died for my sins and rose again to give me everlasting life.

Forgive me for my past, Father, and help me to begin to live a life that glorifies you from this day forward. Fill me with your spirit, Lord, and let me feel the wholeness of being your child.

I thank you for your unconditional love and for accepting me just as I am. God, I choose to never be the same again. Today I am a new creation and I choose to live a life for you.

Thank you for saving me, God.

In Jesus' Name I pray. Amen!

SCRIPTURE REFERENCES:

- 🕊 **John 3:16**
- 🕊 **Romans 10:9-10**
- 🕊 **John 10:10**

DATES

Speaking of dates: Here's a funny story of a date night we went on. We were in Washington, D.C. and decided that we would head to Georgetown and have some hot chocolate. We had such a memorable time on our last date in D.C. sharing hot chocolate, so we tried to recreate that experience. We found ourselves in a quaint little shop, reminiscent of a small French bistro. We ordered our hot chocolate and there we sat, sipping and smiling. Eventually as we continued to sip we both got real quiet and that's when we realized we were hot. I mean real hot. Why the heck were we having hot chocolate when it was 70 degrees outside? We just looked at each other and started laughing.

25 DATE NIGHT IDEAS

- Do something adventurous together.

- Take a salsa class.

- Have a picnic in the living room.

- Have a game night (Our favorite is the game Trouble).

- Go for a walk or hike.

- Take the train just because.

- Have coffee or cocoa on the patio or in the backyard.

- Take an art class.

- Have a movie night at home.

- Get a couple's massage.

- Try a new restaurant.

- Explore an unfamiliar city nearby.

- Revisit the place where you first met.

- Check out an open mic.

- Do karaoke at home or find a karaoke spot in your area.

- Pick strawberries or apples at a local farm.

- Try a drive-in movie.

- Go to a concert.

- Peruse the book store.

- Go to a marriage retreat.

- Run a marathon together.

- Have a spa day.

- Sit outside and count stars/observe constellations.

- Go for a ride.

- Explore a winery.

- Visit a local museum.

- Check out a play.

Bibliography

Cherlin, A. J., Furstenberg,Frank F.,,Jr, & al, e. (1991). Longitudinal studies of effects of divorce on children in great britain and the united states. *Science, 252*(5011), 1386.

Kalter, N. (1987). Long-term effects of divorce on children: A developmental vulnerability model. *American Journal of Orthopsychiatry, 57*(4), 587-600.

Rath, Tom. *Vital Friends: The People You Can't Afford to Live Without* (Gallup Press, 2006).

Acknowledgments

- Bishop Paul Morton and Pastor Debra Morton - www.cagmin.org

- Dr. David Cooper – www.mountparan.com

- Dr. Creflo Dollar and Pastor Taffi Dollar – www.worldchangers.org

- Pastor Jay and Christy Haizlip - mysanctuarychurch.com

- Elizabeth Carroll - www.marriagebootcamp.com

- Heather Lindsey – www.heatherllindsey.com

- Chessette Cowan - cheesettestovallministries.org

- Dale and Tonya Ferguson contribution - https://4littlefergusons.wordpress.com/

- Wedding photos – provided on behalf of couples acknowledging permission by photographer to publish.

About the Authors

M.L. and Arian Moore have a heart for marriage and a desire to inspire other couples to stay committed. They serve as marriage group leaders at their local church. M.L., a native of New Orleans, Louisiana, is a graduate of Oglethorpe University and completed his graduate studies at Liberty University. M.L. is also a U.S. Navy veteran. Arian, an Atlanta, Georgia native, is a graduate of Howard University and completed her graduate studies at Regent University. They reside in the Atlanta area.

Follow them on social media @makethevowkeepthevow. For booking and speaking requests contact modspotmedia@gmail.com

www.ingramcontent.com/pod-product-compliance
Lightning Source LLC
Chambersburg PA
CBHW060928040426
42445CB00011B/846